G H

BE STILL AND KNOW

GEORGIA HARKNESS

BE STILL
AND KNOW

ABINGDON PRESS

NEW YORK   NASHVILLE

FOREWORD

IT WAS IN THE FALL OF 1931 THAT I SUDDENLY DISCOVERED THE joys of writing poetry. A poet friend, Molly Anderson Haley, came to Elmira College, where I was then teaching, to give a two weeks' course in versification. I joined the class out of casual interest, for I had never been able to understand other people's poetry very well and had no idea I could write any. On the first day I wrote a bit of whimsical verse, on the second "Holy Flame." Others followed in close succession. This has convinced me that many persons could write verse if only their inhibitions were released.

My first book of poems, entitled *Holy Flame*, was published by Bruce Humphries, Inc., in 1935. It is now out of print, and some of the poems I like best from it are here rescued from oblivion. Several others have appeared in *The Christian Century, The Christian Advocate*, and *motive*. To the editors of these publications I am indebted for permission to reprint; to the Division of Christian Education of the National Council of Churches of Christ in the U.S.A. for permission to use selections from the Revised Standard Version of the Bible and in a few instances from the American Standard Version. While the prayers are in the free church tradition, the reader will occasionally find phrases not only from Scripture but from the great liturgies of the ages. These I trust are familiar enough to require no identification.

Unlike my earlier volume of poems and prayers, *The Glory of God*, this book has the prayer in each case integrated with the theme of the poem and a brief scripture passage as the setting. It is hoped that this will increase its usefulness both for private and for public worship. If in some measure the book assists its readers to worship the Lord in the beauty of holiness, its purpose will have been fulfilled.

GEORGIA HARKNESS

CONTENTS

CONTENTS

BE STILL AND KNOW

Be still, and know that I am God.—Ps. 46:10

Be still and know
That God is in His world,
Though clouds shut out the light,
Though ghoulish specters stalk,
And all is night.

Be still and know
That God is in His world,
Though Mammon clamors loud,
And Mars lifts flashing steel,
Untamed and proud.

Be still and know
That God is in His world,
Though men with reckless waste
May seek they know not what
In feverish haste.

Be still and know
That God is in His world.
God speaks, but none may hear
That voice except he have
The listening ear.

O God, who art the guard and guide of all who put their trust in Thee, grant us Thy peace. Thou knowest the cares that torment our spirits. Thou seest the way before us more clearly than our eyes can discern it. Forgive the anxieties that cloud our minds and consume our strength; in Thee let us rest and be strong.

Save us, O Lord, from anxious self-concern; from dark imaginings; from distrust of Thy guiding care. Give us wisdom to act and faith to wait. So shall Thy peace which passes understanding be ours. Through Jesus Christ our Lord. AMEN.

SYMBOLS

Open my eyes, that I may behold
wondrous things out of thy law.
I am a sojourner on earth;
hide not thy commandments from me!
—Ps. 119:18-19 (R.S.V.)

If I would penetrate the veil that lies
Between my thought and every human mind,
To follow on where science leads, or find
In vast cathedral towering to the skies
The token of an art that never dies,
To trace in poetry, in faces lined,
In babies' smiles, a meaning clear defined,
Then must I read the symbols, and surmise.

If I would link my questing mind with One
Who contemplates all wisdom, views all art,
Who holds all teeming nature in His hand,
Who sent to earth His love-begotten Son
That men might learn to live with godlike heart,
Then must I read the signs, and understand.

Open Thou our eyes, O Lord, that we may behold wondrous things out of Thy law. Pilgrims and strangers though we be, hide not Thy commandments or Thy presence from us.

We rejoice, O God, that Thou hast made the way so plain that wayfaring men need not grope in darkness. By the beauty and bounty and order of Thy creation, by illumined souls who have caught some vision of Thy truth and have transmitted it to others, by the great heritage of our faith, by Thy Word in our Holy Scriptures, and above all, by Thy blessed Son our Lord, we see Thee in Thy goodness and glory.

Open today our eyes to see Thee; quicken our minds to know Thee; warm our hearts to love Thee; strengthen our hands to serve Thee. Through Jesus Christ our Lord. AMEN.

THE GRAIL

Whither shall I go from thy Spirit?
Or whither shall I flee from thy presence?
—Ps. 139:7 (R.S.V.)

I find Thee, Lord, this springtime afternoon,
In chirp of robin, flowering apple tree,
In virgin green of lawns, fresh, violet-strewn,
In stirring branches' shadowed tracery.
I find Thee, Lord, in children's merry play,
Syntonic to the music of the spheres;
In lovers' eyes, as sunlit as the day;
In old men's faces mellowed with the years.

I find Thee in still temples of the wood;
I find Thee in the pealing of great choirs;
I find Thee in men's strivings toward the good;
I find Thee where my inmost heart aspires.

So radiant Thou, the quest I cannot fail,
For round about me lies the Holy Grail.

O Thou who lovest beauty and hast filled Thy world to fullness with it, we rejoice that Thou hast placed in the loveliness of Thy creation a speaking witness to Thyself. Strip off, O Lord, the impediments that sometimes veil our eyes, and help us in all Thy handiwork to behold Thee.

We would remember, our Father, that Thou art also in the dark places as in those radiant with Thy glory. If we make our bed in hell, Thou art there; if we take the wings of the morning and dwell in the uttermost parts of the sea, even there shall Thy hand lead us, and Thy right hand shall hold us. Even the darkness hideth not from Thee: the darkness and the light are both alike to Thee.

We would behold Thee, Lord, and beholding adore and serve Thee. AMEN.

BE OF GOOD CHEER

And when the disciples saw him walking on the sea, they were troubled, saying, It is a ghost; and they cried out for fear. But straightway Jesus spake unto them, saying, Be of good cheer; it is I; be not afraid.—Matt. 14:26-27 (A.S.V.)

Something there is in Him like surging of great waves
That beat upon the shore with never-ceasing might;
Something there is like radiant flashing spray, that laves
The barren rocks and turns them into things of light.

Something there is like mighty ocean's boundless peace,
Aglow with sunshine after storm-swept nights of fear;
Something there is that brings to storm-swept souls release,
That speaks to troubled mariners: Be of good cheer.

We thank Thee, O God, for the glorious radiance of Thy Son Jesus Christ, who in all His ministry preached good news to the poor, proclaimed release to the captives and recovering of sight to the blind, and set at liberty those who were oppressed.

In the stormy winds of our time, when hearts are despairing and fearful, He speaks to say, "Be of good cheer. I am near thee. Be not afraid." At His words our hearts are lifted up and our strength renewed. Fill Thou our souls today, O Lord, with His joy and peace. AMEN.

14

THE UNDERSTANDING HEART

And behold, a woman of the city, who was a sinner, when she learned that he was sitting at table in the Pharisee's house, brought an alabaster flask of ointment, and standing behind him at his feet, weeping, she began to wet his feet with her tears, and wiped them with the hair of her head, and kissed his feet, and anointed them with the ointment.
—Luke 7:37-38 (R.S.V.)

Give me, O God, the understanding heart—
The quick discernment of the soul to see
Another's inner wish, the hidden part
Of him that, wordless, speaks for sympathy.
I would be kind, but kindness is not all:
In arid places may I find the wells,
The deeps within my neighbor's soul that call
To me, and lead me where his spirit dwells.

When Jesus lifted Mary Magdalene
And Mary came with alabaster flask,
A deed was wrought—but more; and there was seen
The bond of holy love for which I ask.
Give me, O God, the understanding heart
Lit with the quickening flame Thou dost impart.

Almighty and ever-loving God, whose heart is open to all Thy children, whose eye sees all, whose ear is never deaf to our cry, enlarge our compassion. Help us with a holy love akin to Thine to press behind the walls that so often separate troubled, lonely souls from other men. Let us by Thy grace bring to the inner springs of life Thy healing ministry.

Forgive us, Lord, that we are so often insensitive, callous, self-concerned. Tear down the flimsy defenses by which we have sought to wall ourselves from Thee, and knit us to Thyself in firmer, richer fellowship. In Jesus' name. AMEN.

THINK THOU LIKE GOD

But turning and seeing his disciples, he rebuked Peter,
and said, "Get behind me, Satan! For you are not on the side
of God, but of men."

—Mark 8:33 (R.S.V.)

Think thou like God, or hide thyself
  From out My sight;
So shall thy darkness not becloud
  The day with night.

Think thou upon the things of God,
  Not thoughts of men;
So shall a sick and weary world
  Find peace again.

Think thou with Me, and labor in
  The light divine;
So shall thy guerdon be My cross,
  My strength be thine.

O God of holiness, unto whom the thoughts and intents of all
hearts are known, grant that with repentance and true godliness
we may think Thy thoughts after Thee. Help us to strip away
the masks by which we have thought to hide from Thee; in the
clear light of Thy righteousness show us our sin.

O Lord, by Thy forgiving mercy take from us the pride and
self-seeking, the envy and anger, the hurtfulness to other men
and·dullness to Thee, by which we have done evil in Thy sight.
Grant that from this day forth in renewal of spirit and steadfastness of devotion we may find in Thee peace for living and
strength for serving. Through Christ our Lord. AMEN.

16

ADVERSITY

My Father, if it be possible, let this cup pass from me; nevertheless, not as I will, but as thou wilt.
　　　　　　　　　　　　—Matt. 26:39 (R.S.V.)

When I reflect upon the ills of life,
The storms that rack the sturdiest souls with pain,
Strong spirits warped and crushed beneath the strain
Of poverty, ill health, disaster, strife,
And all the myriad evils that are rife
In human kind, that fall like sullen rain
On good and bad, on high and low, that drain
Man's finite strength and cut with cosmic knife:
Then am I stirred to ask, "Why is it so?
Is there no God of love? Does He not care?"
And as I ponder thus, my wit undone,
A voice that spoke two thousand years ago
Comes echoing to me from a garden prayer,
Triumphant, "Not my will, but Thine, be done."

O God, who hast been our dwelling place in all generations, support and direct us still. In a world aglow with Thy beauty, the whole creation yet groaneth and travaileth together in pain. Without Thee we perish.

Guard us, O Lord, from regarding as Thy holy will the miseries wrought by the sin and indifference of men. Help us to labor with Thee to banish needless suffering. But guard us also from shrinking from pain when it comes in the path of duty or within the ordering of Thy world. Help us to change what we can and to endure what we must, knowing that pain can teach us much and that in everything Thou dost work for good with those who love Thee.

We thank Thee, blessed Lord, for the example and the saving power of Him who, facing the cross, could still trust and follow Thee. Help us ever in our small Gethsemanes to say with Him, "Not my will, but Thine, be done." AMEN.

GOD SUFFERS

Surely he has borne our griefs
and carried our sorrows; . . .
But he was wounded for our transgressions,
he was bruised for our iniquities.
—Isa. 53:4-5 (R.S.V.)

I cannot think that God could be content
To view unmoved the toiling and the strain,
The groaning of the ages, sick and spent,
The whole creation travailing in pain.
The suffering God is no vast cosmic force,
That by some blind, unthinking, loveless power
Keeps stars and atoms swinging in their course,
And reckons naught of men in this grim hour.
Nor is the suffering God a fair ideal
That comes to birth within a valiant heart,
A figment of the mind to help me steel
My soul to pain and play a manly part.
God suffers with a love that cleanses dross;
A God like that, I see upon a cross.

Almighty God, unto whom all hearts are open, Thou knowest the sinful, sorrowing hearts of men. And Thou who knowest all hast come among us in Thy blessed Son to bear our griefs, to carry our sorrows, to heal the wounds of our transgressions! We thank Thee, Lord.

The manifold quests of the human mind to find Thee, O God, bear witness that Thou hast made us for Thyself. But in Jesus Christ Thou hast made Thyself so manifest that we need no other sign! In His ministry of suffering love and His death for our redemption we see Thy Father-heart. By His living presence Thou dost ever comfort and sustain us. As in Him Thou dost bear our griefs and forgive our iniquities, so help us to give our lives to Thee in full devotion. Through Jesus Christ our Lord. AMEN.

THE DARK

If I say, Surely the darkness shall overwhelm me,
And the light about me shall be night;
Even the darkness hideth not from thee,
But the night shineth as the day:
The darkness and the light are both alike to thee.
                                    —Ps. 139:11-12 (A.S.V.)

The dark—
" 'Tis midnight; and on Olive's brow"
The purest of all sons of men
Accepts a cross to save my spirit now
From midnight's gloom because He bore it then.

The dark—
Within its grasp a world is caught,
Engulfed in pain, with yawning rifts of fear.
Because in love and beauty God hath wrought
A light shines through the dark to bless and cheer.

Enlighten, O God, our darkness, that beholding Thee we may
dwell in confidence, trusting Thee we may not be confounded,
serving Thee we may be used for the furtherance of Thy Kingdom and the doing of Thy will among men. Through Christ our
Lord. AMEN.

19

EXILE

He giveth power to the faint; and to them that have no might he increaseth strength. Even the youths shall faint and be weary, and the young men shall utterly fall: but they that wait upon the Lord shall renew their strength; they shall mount up with wings as eagles; they shall run, and not be weary; and they shall walk, and not faint.—Isa. 40:29-31

"They that wait upon the Lord renew their strength;
On eagles' wings they mount up to the skies;
When in the race they scan the highway's length
They faint not, and unwearied, gain the prize."
In Babylon men heard a prophet's voice,
Afire with God's supernal majesty.
Amid their tears they could again rejoice:
They heard him say, "My people, comfort ye!"

No exile has been mine, save that I made.
My soul moved out and left the holy fires;
No conquering armies, but a deepening shade
Hid from my sight the gleaming temple spires.
And when I yearned for home, I heard God say,
"Wait ye upon the Lord, and find the way."

God of all comfort, our Refuge and Strength, forgive us the weakness we need not have, the weariness we bring upon ourselves, the dullness into which we fall through our own folly and neglect. When the infirmities of the flesh assail us, we know that Thou wilt heal or give us power to endure. But when the deep waters engulf our souls, too often we despair and turn away from Thy proffered hand.

Save and deliver us, O Lord, from that dark night in which we feel ourselves to be lonely exiles in a strange land. Renew our strength as we wait before Thee, that by Thy grace we may mount up with wings, run and not be weary, walk and not faint. And to Thee we shall give the praise of grateful hearts. AMEN.

WAS I MADE TO DIE?

Yea, though I walk through the valley of the shadow of death, I will fear no evil: for thou art with me; thy rod and thy staff they comfort me. —Ps. 23:4

Poets, prophets, priests, and sages
Probe the veil throughout the ages.
Yet thick the curtain hangs.
Death comes to all. Its pangs
Confound alike the great and lowly,
Untutored soul, or wise and holy.
Was I made to die?
No clear light have I.

Unseeking came I here.
I live, but not in fear.
Tomorrow's future is uncertain:
Before the daybreak hangs a curtain.
I sleep; no shadows lurk;
I shall arise and work.
I need no light to reach the morrow:
Why then torment my soul with sorrow?

No troubled, fearing mind can keep
Vigil over death or sleep.
Faith can greet the veil.
God lives! Then what avail
Has fruitless fear or idle care?
Sleep, my soul, arise and dare!
This knowledge have we all,
No evil can befall.

Father, we know that in the shadow of Thy great protection no evil can befall us, either in life or after death. Help us then to put our hands in Thine and go into the darkness unafraid. AMEN.

THOUGHTS ON LIFE AND DEATH

The Lord gave, and the Lord hath taken away; blessed be the name of the Lord. —Job 1:21

> My body is not mine. As at the inn
> I have "my room"—"my bed"—and there within
> Its borrowed warmth I rest as if 'twere owned.
> So is this flesh not mine to mar, but loaned.[1]
>
> . . . .
>
> As falls the ripened olive from the tree
> When sap is stayed,
> So may Death find me thanking God for life,
> And unafraid.[2]
>
> . . . .
>
> As fronts the promontory to the waves
> And tames the sea amid the surging din,
> So stands the life firm fashioned in the deeps,
> All nature lies beneath, and God within.[3]

Lord of heaven and earth, who dost hold in Thy gracious care both the living and the dead, we bring to Thee in loving remembrance those dear to us who have passed beyond our sight. We thank Thee for their winsome lives, for the inspiration of their friendship, for the imperishable bonds by which they are knit to us. For happy memories of little acts of kindness, for remembrance of work and play and laughter and song together, for glad rejoicing in their fellowship, we give Thee grateful thanks.

Hold them, O God, close to Thee in Thine eternal kingdom. Help us to live more nobly because Thou hast given them to us, and when at the last Thou dost call us to Thyself, grant that we may meet Thee untroubled and unafraid. AMEN.

[1] Epictetus *Discourses* I. 24.
[2] Marcus Aurelius *Meditations* IV. 48.
[3] *Ibid.* IV. 49.

I THANK HIM STILL

Be thankful unto him, and bless his name. For the Lord is good; his mercy is everlasting. —Ps. 100:4-5

I thank my God for sleep—
And when I cannot sleep, I thank Him still
For waking dreams, for fantasies that fill
The night with pleasant converse; witchery
Of happy hours now vanished; alchemy
That turns the leaden night to burnished gold.
Within this waking dream-world I behold
The friends I shall not see by morning's light;
They traverse continents and come by night
Across the years to live in memory.

I thank Him too for fancies playing sportively,
Like sunshine, on tomorrow's good brown earth—
For sparkling waves, and flowers brought to birth
While still the winter's frost comes stealing in;
For warmth of body, peace of heart within;
For waking rest, and trusting confidence
That underneath my soul is sure defense
And naught from out the night can bring me ill.

I thank my God for sleep—
And when I cannot sleep, I thank Him still.

O Thou Giver of all that is good, we thank Thee for Thy mercies, new every morning and fresh every evening, and more than we can number. Thou hast given us the succession of day and night, and ordainest good purposes for both the darkness and the light. Thou givest us work to do and after it refreshment of body and renewal of soul. We thank Thee, Lord.

Help us as we lay our bodies down to place our spirits in Thy keeping, assured that Thou art ever near and in Thee is our peace. Through our Lord Christ we pray. AMEN.

SECURITY

God is our refuge and strength,
a very present help in trouble.
Therefore we will not fear though the earth should change,
though the mountains shake in the heart of the sea;
though its waters roar and foam,
though the mountains tremble with its tumult.

—Ps. 46:1-3 (R.S.V.)

As falls the rain a thousand miles away
And by its gift a teeming Nile is fed;
As miracle of spring creeps on each day
And by the lode of distant sun is led;
As currents deep from out a lengthening past
Are caught and harnessed by a mighty dam:
So do world-rooted tendrils hold me fast,
Deep unto deep, to make me what I am.

Almighty God, Creator of heaven and earth, in Thee is our security. We thank Thee for the great stabilities of Thy world, which even in the midst of turmoil and change reveal Thy handiwork in ordered unity. We thank Thee for seedtime and harvest, for cold and heat, for summer and winter, for day and night, which shall not cease while the earth remaineth. Still more we thank Thee for the ties that bind us to our human kind—for family and friends; for childhood and youth, maturity and age; for a great heritage provided for us by those who have gone before.

But above all we thank Thee for Thy fatherly hand, which never fails. Thou art with us in sickness and health, in abundance and want, in joy and sorrow, in times of war and in days of peace. Thou art our Refuge and Strength, our ever-present Help. In Thee we trust. AMEN.

ARTISTRY

How lovely is thy dwelling place,
O Lord of hosts!
—Ps. 84:1 (R.S.V.)

In the peace of God I rest,
Knowing that out of strife
The Master-Artist of us all
 Is forming life.

He makes His hand-craft gleam
With radiance unlent,
For not with stark utility
 Is God content.

He makes majestic hills,
And sea-gulls flying low,
The calm content of rippling waves
 And sunset glow.

He makes men strong to dare,
And souls that smile through pain.
He touches life with holy joy
 In glad refrain.

So in His life I rest,
Upborne and unafraid,
Assured such artistry must change,
 Can never fade.

We rejoice, O Thou Maker of heaven and earth, that Thou hast made Thy dwelling place and ours so lovely. In all Thy world is seen the touch of Thy master hand. Our hearts overflow; our cup of joy runs over. But in Thy sons and daughters is still fairer evidence of Thy handiwork. For beauty of soul in those whose lives have blessed ours we praise Thee.

Work Thou, O Lord, Thine artistry upon us as we lie still before Thee. And to Thee shall all the glory be given. AMEN.

WONDER

Thine, O Lord, is the greatness, and the power, and the glory, and the victory, and the majesty; for all that is in the heaven and in the earth is thine. —I Chron. 29:11

To stand tiptoe before a Christmas tree,
Sparkling and wonderful, aglow with light,
To feel new worlds unfold before one's sight
And silent rapture strive with speaking glee—
This is akin to what the mystics see
At rending of the veil, when beauty bright,
New and ineffable, with quickening might
O'erfloods the life with awe and ecstasy.

The splendor of God's presence I have felt
Where great cathedrals speak throughout all time;
Where torrents roar in cataracts of wild,
Unstaying, ceaseless power: at sunrise knelt
Before His radiance, flaming and sublime—
And felt the sudden wonder of a child.

Lord of mystery and marvel, Thou knowest us altogether. Thou understandest our thoughts; Thou art acquainted with all our ways. But before the mystery of Thy splendor we are mute. Such knowledge is too wonderful for us; it is high; we cannot attain to it.

Only to praise Thee from a glad heart would we break silence as we stand before Thee. Like the singers of Israel we could cry out with fullness of joy, "Let every thing that hath breath praise the Lord! Praise ye the Lord!"

Give us, O God, at times the raptured wonder of a child; then through our days the steadied insights of maturity. But always let us praise Thee. AMEN.

TO MUSIC

*Praise him with the sound of the trumpet: praise him
with the psaltery and harp. Praise him with the timbrel and
dance: praise him with stringed instruments and organs. . . .
Let every thing that hath breath praise the Lord. Praise ye
the Lord.* —Ps. 150:3-4, 6

Rippling, flashing wavelets of sound,
Angels dancing on holy ground:
Deep, sonorous diapasons;
Priests intoning their orisons;
Old refrains from a violin,
Piercing the ruck of earthborn din;
Orchestral tumult or high, clear note,
Liquid gold from an artist's throat;
Joyous carol, rollicking song
Giving cheer when the day is long—
Music is Heaven's gift to sorrow,
So play and sing for a glad tomorrow!

We bless Thee, O God, that Thou hast placed in the hearts of
men and women and little children the impulse to make music.
By manifold instruments devised by the art of men and by that
greatest of instruments, the human voice in song, our souls are
stirred to purer and more joyous living. We thank Thee, Lord.

By music men have praised Thee in all times and in all places.
By music we proclaim our adoration beyond the power of our
poor words to speak. By music hearts are knit together in common
joyous praise to Thee. We thank thee, Lord.

If perchance Thou hast imparted to us some power to make
melody, help us to stir up the gift that is in us and to use it
to Thy glory. Through Christ our Lord. AMEN.

TO BEAUTY

He has made everything beautiful in its time; also he has put eternity into man's mind.   —Eccl. 3:11 (R.S.V.)

To catch the soul's upsurge that beauty lends
To questing minds—pulse quickened, life made new,
Then must I learn to listen, find new friends
In all God's world, and let the light shine through.

. . . .

"Pain is a passing thing, but beauty lives,"
So spoke a soul who, bound by body's chains,
Wrought valiantly. As dies the seed that gives
New life, pain passes but the fruit remains.

. . . .

To view the sea of beauty, vast and fair,
And on its shores grow strong and keen of sight—
This is to see, in time, eternal light
And learn to know one beauty everywhere.

O God, who hast filled Thy world with beauty and kindled the love of it in the hearts of men, quicken our minds and open our eyes to find it. Strip away the impediments of self-will and of concern with petty, humdrum matters that so often veil our sight, and give us the vision splendid. Help us amid pain of body or tribulation of soul to lift up our eyes to behold what is beautiful, and beyond it to behold Thee in Thy glory.

O Thou who hast set eternity in our hearts, let us not prove recreant to this high calling. Enlarge our horizons and widen the sweep of our lives until in all things we behold Thy goodness, Thy truth, Thy beauty, Thy holiness. AMEN.

BLESSED—

Blessed are the poor in spirit, for theirs is the kingdom of heaven. —Matt. 5:3 (R.S.V.)

I

Blessed are the poor in spirit,
Who proclaim not their virtue,
But humbly own their sin and seek release;

Who condemn not in haste,
But hold their peace that all may dwell in peace;

Who seal not their hearts,
But let God's presence give their cares surcease;
Blessed are they,
For theirs is the kingdom of heaven.

O God our Father, we lift to Thee our grateful praise. Thou art our strong Deliverer. In hours of darkness Thou hast been our Support; in joy our Companion. From Thy hand comes every good gift. For family and friends, for beauty and laughter, for work and prayer, we give Thee thanks. Above all we thank Thee for the gift of Thy blessed Son for our redemption.

Forgive, O Lord, the littleness of our return for Thy great bounty. Save and deliver us from the sins that so easily beset us—our selfishness, our pride, our anxiety, our envy, our eagerness to be praised, our resentments, our unkindness, our narrowness of vision, our complacency before the world's suffering and great need.

Create in us clean hearts, O God, and renew a right spirit within us. AMEN.

BLESSED—

Blessed are those who mourn, for they shall be comforted.
                                    —Matt. 5:4 (R.S.V.)

2

Blessed are they that mourn,
Who pity not themselves,
But weep with those whose grief they would console;

Who flaunt not their sorrow,
But greet with calm the storm that takes its toll,

Who rail not at pain,
But find in it God's tonic to the soul;
Blessed are they,
For they shall be comforted.

Father of mercies and God of all comfort, speak through the world's distress Thy word of triumph over pain. Help us to know that whatever befalls us Thou art our great Companion, our fellow sufferer who understands.

Grant Thy presence to those who today suffer grievously—the fearful, the lonely, the defeated, the oppressed, the bereaved, and those who are weary and sick in body, mind, or soul. Grant unto them a deep and sure conviction that neither life, nor death, nor things present, nor things to come, nor anything else in all creation shall be able to separate them from Thy love and care.

O God, deliver us from evil—from pain if it may be, but always from sin. Help us to take up our crosses and follow Thee, and if the path to which Thou callest be in a dark valley, help us to walk in it bravely with Thee. Through Christ our Lord. AMEN.

BLESSED—

Blessed are the meek, for they shall inherit the earth.
                              —Matt. 5:5 (R.S.V.)

3

Blessed are the meek,
Who seek not wealth,
But lay up treasures of a fairer kind;

Who seek not power,
But are content with conquests of the mind;

Who seek not fame,
But let their deeds a worthful guerdon find;
Blessed are they,
For they shall inherit the earth.

O God, from whose hand cometh every good gift, and who hast not called us to lay up earthly riches but to seek heavenly treasures, give us true discernment. Grant that in simplicity of living and in purity of heart we may be stripped of all impediments and made strong for Thee. Help us in gratitude to use to Thy honor and service the goods with which Thou hast endowed us. Enable us in all our successes to give Thee alone the glory, and in time of failure to remember that Thou still art near. Restore unto us daily the joy of Thy salvation, and uphold us with a willing spirit. So may we be used as Thou desirest for the advancement of Thy kingdom and the service of the world. Through Jesus Christ our Lord. AMEN.

BLESSED—

Blessed are those who hunger and thirst for righteousness, for they shall be satisfied. —Matt. 5:6 (R.S.V.)

4

Blessed are they that hunger and thirst after
   righteousness,
Who yearn not for gold,
But find in God a power to banish greed;

Who hunger not for food,
But have enough to satisfy their need;

Who thirst not for drink
But drink of living waters as their meed;
Blessed are they,
For they shall be filled.

O God, our help in ages past, our hope for years to come, grant unto us now cleansing from sin and newness of life in Thee. Purge us, we pray, of our selfishness, our self-righteous pride, our anger and envy, our narrowness of outlook, our indifference to the feelings and needs of others, our dullness and indifference to Thee. We deserve not the mercy that in love Thou hast promised through Thy blessed Son, but in faith and repentance we beseech Thee for it.

Give us Thy Spirit, Lord, to triumph over temptation. Fill us, we pray, with Thy grace and power that we may go and sin no more, and that we may ever hereafter serve and please Thee in newness of life to the honor and glory of Thy holy name. Through Jesus Christ our Lord. AMEN.

BLESSED—

Blessed are the merciful, for they shall obtain mercy.
                                    —Matt.5:7 (R.S.V.)

5

Blessed are the merciful,
Who scorn not the poor,
But hear the cry of those who want for bread;

Who neglect not the sick,
But bind their wounds, bring healing to their bed;

Who despise not the weak,
But see in these the face of God instead;
Blessed are they,
For they shall obtain mercy.

We confess before Thee, O God, the littleness of our faith and of our sympathy. Amid the comfort and security with which Thou hast blessed our lives, our hearts have been dull before the agony of the world. Forgive us, O Lord.

Speak Thou Thy word of victory over evil. Comfort all who mourn. Heal those who are sick in body or soul. Care for the destitute and the bereaved. Guide those who are perplexed. Be near the lonely. Knit Thy children everywhere into a closer fellowship. Give wisdom and courage to those who hold in their hands the destinies of nations, and stir in Thy people a will to dwell together in compassion and understanding love. So shall Thy kingdom come and Thy will be done on earth. Through Jesus Christ our Lord. AMEN.

BLESSED—

Blessed are the pure in heart, for they shall see God.
— Matt. 5:8 (R.S.V.)

6

Blessed are the pure in heart,
Who envy not the strong,
But grow in strength themselves from inner springs;

Who defile not their speech,
But put away the lewd, the oath that stings;

Who lust not within,
But keep a holy love for holy things;
Blessed are they,
For they shall see God.

O God most holy, whose thoughts are not our thoughts and whose ways are not our ways, teach us to think Thy thoughts after Thee and to walk in Thy ways.

Make us and preserve us, Lord, clean in body, mind, and spirit. Guard our tongues from bearing evil report, and our lips from unclean speech. Help us to subdue the impulses of the flesh, that in cleanness of living and control of bodily appetites we may be strong to do Thy holy will. Give us the purity of heart that thinks no evil, that rejoices not in iniquity but rejoices in the truth. Lord Christ, be Thou in temptation, our light, our guide, our strong defense. AMEN.

BLESSED—

Blessed are the peacemakers, for they shall be called sons of God. —Matt. 5:9 (R.S.V.)

7

Blessed are the peacemakers,
Who love not strife,
But find their joy in fellowship and mirth;

Who provoke not wrath,
But quench the grievous word that gives it birth;

Who bless not war,
But lift a voice to banish it from earth;
Blessed are they,
For they shall be called sons of God.

We pray Thee, Lord, for peace. As the angels sang of Thy glory and of peace on earth, good will toward men, so let this word be fulfilled in our time.

Sustain with Thy presence all who labor for peace and justice. Advance the spirit of reconciling love. Help us to discern the grave responsibilities of our time and to perform them with integrity. Impart to all rulers and governors the will and the wisdom to guide their people into paths of peace.

Be very near to those who are caught in the toils of war, and if it be possible, give them a speedy issue from their sufferings. And let us who dwell in comfort while others bear the burden of the nations' strife be spurred to nobler effort that peace may come. In the name of our Christ. AMEN.

BLESSED—

*Blessed are those who are persecuted for righteousness'
sake, for theirs is the kingdom of heaven.*
—Matt. 5:10 (R.S.V.)

8

Blessed are they that are persecuted for right-
  eousness' sake,
Who suffer not for sin,
But bear the stigma in a righteous task;

Who quail not at scorn,
But face the world's disdain and wear no mask;

Who yield not to defeat,
But find a cross the high reward they ask;
Blessed are they,
For theirs is the kingdom of heaven.

We thank Thee, blessed Lord, for that great company of saints,
apostles, prophets, martyrs, who have been persecuted for righteousness' sake. Because they failed Thee not and were faithful even
unto death, we have entered into a great heritage of faith. As Thou
hast given them a crown of life in Thy heavenly kingdom, so may
Thy kingdom on earth go forward in us through our fidelity to
their witness.

Deliver us, we pray, from the temptation to pride ourselves on
false or little martyrdoms. May our bearing of Thy cross be to Thy
glory only, and to the service of men without expectation of reward.

When Thou dost call us into ways of suffering for righteousness' sake, walk with us in the way and give boldness to our speech
and our decisions. Help us to follow Thee and to trust Thee unto
the uttermost. For Christ's sake. AMEN.

TIDINGS

My soul magnifies the Lord,
and my spirit rejoices in God my Savior.
—Luke 1:46-47 (R.S.V.)

Through all the years the tidings have been spread,
Of how there came to one of low estate
A harbinger of joy—how Mary said,
"My soul doth magnify the Lord, for great
And holy is His name." The star, the light,
The shepherds, wise men bringing spice and gold,
The heavenly host that caroled in the night—
This is the tale that never can grow old.

"To God give glory; let peace reign on earth!"
They heard and wondered. Could these words be life?
A glimpse of truth supernal at the birth
Of Him who came to free the world of strife?
And still men wonder. But the humble hear,
And find in Him the love that conquers fear.

We thank Thee, blessed Lord, that Thou hast not reserved Thy gifts for the great ones of the earth but visitest the humble. When in love Thou didst send to earth Thy best Gift for our salvation, Thou didst speak glad tidings to Thy handmaiden of low estate. Like Mary we would magnify Thee, for our spirits rejoice in God our Saviour. Like Mary, though no such high calling be ours, we would hear and heed the word Thou hast for us.

Lord of heaven and earth, let Christ be born anew within our hearts today. This is our prayer; we need no more. AMEN.

HERITAGE

And Jesus increased in wisdom and in stature, and in fa-
vor with God and man. —Luke 2:52 (R.S.V.)

In Nazareth, a simple country town,
A child grew up. He was a Jewish boy
Whom none supposed would come to great renown,
Though all the neighbors loved him for his joy
In birds and flowers, his eager, thoughtful care
Of old and sick, his diligence to get
The wisdom that the sacred books declare.
They smiled and said, "He'll be a rabbi yet!"

At twelve a great adventure came. He went
On journey to Jerusalem. All eyes
To see the temple, ears to hear, he spent
The precious hours in questioning the wise.
He had to be there in God's house, why not?
The day soon passed: it never was forgot.

O God our all-wise and loving Father, we rejoice that Thou hast
placed in the heart of every child the impulse to learn, to grow,
to reach out and grasp his world. When Thou camest in human
flesh to dwell among men, Thou didst not depart from this chosen
way. We are glad that the lad of Nazareth, moved by this eager
stirring, was thus led to the maturing of His mind and soul. Show
us how to help all children to grow in wisdom and stature and
in favor with God and man. And as He entered into His heritage,
so may we be quickened and made more faithful to that heritage
of faith and truth in which He stands as Thy great Revealer. In
His name we pray. AMEN.

TEMPTATION

*You shall worship the Lord your God
and him only shall you serve.*

—Matt. 4:10 (R.S.V.)

The Father's Son was tempted once, as I—
For naught that men must suffer could He shun—
That time a voice had spoken from on high
To witness, "This is my beloved son,
In whom I am well pleased." And could it be
That He of all God's sons was thus endowed
With strength and favor? Might it not be He—
The King to lift again a people proud
Of lineage, the chosen of the Lord?
Such musings caught His mind; they would not down.
Thus might He serve, and still might gain reward
Of bread, great kingdoms, glory and renown.

He faced these spectres, vanquished them, and came
Back to His kin to love men in God's name.

"In him was life; and the life was the light of men." We rejoice,
O God, that as Thy light shone in Him, it still shines in the darkness, and the darkness has not overcome it.

Help us, O Lord, by the power of Thy sinless Son to live in our
time with clean hearts and a right spirit. Give strength for the
daily task, and help us to see each duty, however small, as a service
done for Thee. Let us feel Thee near in whatever may befall us.
Thou knowest our temptations; give us Thy grace. Thou knowest
our cares; grant us Thy peace. Knit us together in love and in
labor, and use us by Thy spirit for the healing of the nations.

To Thy keeping, our Father, we commit ourselves and all we
hold dear. Guard us; guide us; do with us as Thou wilt. In Christ's
name. AMEN.

ENLARGEMENT

God that made the world and all things therein . . . hath made of one blood all nations of men for to dwell on all the face of the earth. —Acts 17:24, 26

From Galilee there went a questing youth
To find in foreign borders solitude:
There He would muse upon the age-old truth
Of God's great plan. And in this interlude
A woman of Phoenicia came in need
To this young Hebrew, called to serve His kin.
Love-drawn she came; her daughter must be freed;
No racial bars could wall God's healing in.

And there upon this Jew, on Mary's son,
There broke new light. To none could He refrain
From gift of self. He saw all men as one,
His God the Lord of all who seek in pain.

Today who seeks to know His healing grace,
Like Him, finds God in fellowship of race.

God the Father almighty, Maker of heaven and earth, in shame we confess before Thee our pride of race and nation, our unholy divisions, our denial of the good things of life to our brothers, Thy sons. Thou who hast made us all of one blood, forgive us our sin. Help us in true repentance to extend our vistas, to break down barriers, to widen the sweep of our love.

We thank Thee, O God, for the way Thy blessed Son has led us. May His compassion for all men be ours. May His fellowship with the humble, the outcast, the alien, teach us to find Thee and serve Thee beyond the borders of our narrow human distinctions. Enlarge our souls, our Father, that our ministry be enlarged. Through Christ our Lord. AMEN.

NOTHING SMALL

Look at the birds of the air. . . . Consider the lilies of the field. . . . Let the children come to me, and do not hinder them; for to such belongs the kingdom of heaven.
— Matt. 6:26, 28; 19:14 (R.S.V.)

In God's creation there was nothing small.
Red sunsets, lilies, sparrows, drag-nets, sheep,
Lost coins, the leaven, mustard seed, and all
The humble daily things of life could keep
The soul alert to understand God's way.
He truly loved the outcast and the poor.
He met a woman at a well one day,
Asked for a drink, then talked, and with a sure,
Swift insight slaked her hidden inner thirst.
An alabaster cruse another brought;
He took her gift of love and placed it first
Before all else this treasure might have bought.
He loved the children—took them on His knee,
Blessed them and said, "Of such God's realm must be!"

O God our loving Father, quicken in us a more Christlike devotion, a more fruitful service, a more discerning mind. As Thy Son our Lord came not to be ministered unto but to minister, help us in His name to be kind to the lonely, the discouraged, the unloved, the sinful, the anxious and sorrowing, and to all Thy little ones. As He saw into the hearts of men and women and little children, kindling them to brighter flame, so wilt Thou give us the understanding heart. Endue us with His breadth of vision and depth of soul, that we may be used by Thee for the advancement of Thy kingdom and the increase of goodness in our world. In His name. AMEN.

DEMONS

Then people went out to see what had happened, and they came to Jesus, and found the man from whom the demons had gone, sitting at the feet of Jesus, clothed and in his right mind. —Luke 8:35 (R.S.V.)

Among the tombs of Gadara there dwelt
A man unclothed, whose spirit was possessed.
Once he had been as other men, and felt
The joys of toil and love. Now sore distressed,
He burst his bands and cut himself with stones.
Men shrank away aghast and left him there,
Until One came whose spirit yet dethrones
The demon things that rend the soul, and tear
The mind apart. He spoke; the devils fled;
The maniac again was clothed and whole.
I know not how He wrought. I think He fed
The thirsty places in the madman's soul.
With His calm radiance He put to rout
The demons, and drove fear and passion out.

O God of purity and peace, who through Thy blessed Son hast taught us the way to strong and ordered living, grant that in control of body, mind, and will we may find in Thee sanity and strength. Make us clean within, that we may be fit dwelling places of Thy Spirit.

Give us, O Lord, the gift of sympathy and an understanding heart. Help us to be bearers of Thy peace and power to those who are sick in body or spirit. Guard our tongues from evil or careless words; teach us how to speak and what deeds of love to do. Let the tensions that in our time tear lives asunder be eased by the spread of mutual helpfulness and reconciling love. Lord Christ, be thou our peace, our light, our joy. AMEN.

LORD, I BELIEVE

Lord, I believe; help thou mine unbelief.—Mark 9:24

"Lord, I believe; help thou mine unbelief,"
So cried a father burdened for his son.
He came to Jesus overborne with grief:
The load was lifted and the victory won.

Today across the lands the anguished cry
Goes up to God, "How long, O Lord, how long?
When wilt Thou save Thy people? Draw Thou nigh—
My son is sore distressed. Lord, make him strong."

Anxious and troubled I believe—and doubt—
But still that calm voice speaks across the years,
"By prayer alone this demon cometh out:
Entrust to Me thy care and loose thy fears."

In Thee, O Lord, I rest and find relief:
Lord, I believe; help Thou mine unbelief.

Lord of heaven and earth, in whose hand are the issues of life and of death, we are silent before the mystery of Thy world. Sickness and tribulation assail pure souls; evil men seem often to wax strong and to prosper while the good are too soon cut off. That these things should be is beyond our understanding, and our faith is not always strong.

We see as in a mirror dimly. But there is light in the healing love of Thy Son our Christ! Help us to believe that in Him is healing for ourselves and those we love, and in His way of love there is healing for the nations. Guard and strengthen those who too young must bear the strains of war, and if it be possible, bring them speedily in safety to their homes. And if they return not, let our grief be transfigured by the faith that by Thy grace death is the open doorway into a larger and more glorious life with Thee. Through Christ our Lord. AMEN.

TRANSFIGURATION

And after six days Jesus took with him Peter and James and John his brother, and led them up a high mountain apart. And he was transfigured before them, and his face shone like the sun. —Matt. 17:1-2 (R.S.V.)

Transfigured on a mount the Master stood,
His raiment white, and dazzling to the sight
In radiance divine. It would be good
To stay and dwell forever in that light,
So Peter thought—but Jesus spake him nay.
He knew that all about was work to do,
That in the vale below a sick boy lay,
And troubled folk they might bring healing to.

I too have seen a vision on a mount—
Have gazed on dazzling whiteness, and been swept
By mountain winds, dew-cleansed at morning's fount.
I yearned to linger there—but downward crept
A mist, and drove me to the vale below.
Because He went, I was less loath to go.

Blessed Lord, who hast called us out of darkness into Thy marvelous light, let now Thy light shine upon us that men may know that we have been with Thee. Help us to walk as children of light, and let the fruit of that light be found in all that is good and right and true.

Quicken our souls, O Lord, to serve Thee in the hard, unlighted paths where dwell Thy needy ones. Help us to carry the glow of the mountaintop into the duties of the plain, and let all of life be transfigured by the light that shone in Jesus Christ. In His name we pray. AMEN.

44

LAST SUPPER

The Lord Jesus on the night when he was betrayed took bread, and when he had given thanks, he broke it, and said, "This is my body which is broken for you. Do this in remembrance of me." —I Cor. 11:23-24 (R.S.V.)

That fateful Thursday night the Master spoke
With His disciples in an upper room.
The twelve most loved were there, and as they broke
Their bread a-quiver at impending doom,
He uttered parting cheer. He bade them give
Obedience to His words, as friendship's sign,
To dwell in love and show men how to live,
To be as branches of the Father's vine.

"Lord, whither goest Thou?" said Peter then.
"My children, where I go thou canst not now."
"To death I follow thee!" he cried again;
But sadness overshadowed Jesus' brow,
Knowing their human frailty—that the test
Would find them sleeping who had loved Him best.

Almighty God, our loving and gracious Father, we come before Thee to confess the shame of our betrayal, to beseech Thy forgiveness, to render to Thee grateful hearts for Thy unfailing mercy.

We are not worthy, O Lord, to claim Thy forgiveness, for like the Twelve we have forsaken Thy Son and departed from His way. We have slept when we ought to have tarried with Him; we have denied Him by idle words and sinful deeds. Forgive us, Lord, and grant that from this day forth we may live in the fellowship of His sufferings and in the power of His triumph over sin and death. Through Christ who died for us. AMEN.

THE BETRAYER

When it was evening, he sat at table with the twelve disciples; and as they were eating, he said, "Truly, I say to you, one of you will betray me." And they were very sorrowful, and began to say to him one after another, "Is it I, Lord?" —Matt. 26:20-22 (R.S.V.)

Upon the outskirts of the surging crowd
He stood transfixed. His brow was white with fear.
He seemed as one struck dumb. Was that a tear
That crept unheeded down his lined face, cowed
With shame and terror? "Yes, I once was proud
To keep the purse," he mused, "and to be near
Him as we sat at meat. Then for a mere
Nothing, for thirty coins—" He wept aloud.

"That kiss!" he moaned. "I did not play him fair.
We dipped together in the dish. That kiss!"
"What ails him? Is he mad?" the people said.
They looked around. He was no longer there.
"Small loss," they sneered. "Some crazy fellow this—
There's more room now." That night they found him
dead.

Lord of all holiness, our hearts are pierced with horror at the betrayal of Thy Son by one of His near and trusted followers. Yet must we also ask, "Lord, is it I?" For we too have betrayed Him. We have sinned against Thee and the calling of Thy Son our Christ. By our self-will and self-seeking, our greed of gain and glory, our envy and jealousy, our pride and anger, our hardness of heart, our lusts of the flesh or graver lusts of the spirit, we have sinned against Thy holy will and betrayed our Master.

Forgive us, we pray Thee, O God. By Thy mercy and not of our own merit, cleanse us from our sins, strengthen us to do Thy will, and help us henceforth to lead lives of purity and steadfastness. Through Jesus Christ our Lord. Amen.

CONQUEST

Pilate said to them, "Then what shall I do with Jesus who is called Christ?" They all said, "Let him be crucified." And he said, "Why, what evil has he done?" But they shouted all the more, "Let him be crucified."

—Matt. 27:22-23 (R.S.V.)

The holy city seethed with murmuring.
A Galilean Jew aspired to sit
On David's throne, they said, and be a king
To rival Caesar. 'Twas the sum of it,
Though when he made this claim, or how, none knew.
"He seems a harmless sort, for so much fuss"—
"You know you never can quite trust a Jew"—
"Away with him! His kind is dangerous!"
The cries grew shriller, and the mob prevailed.

They nailed Him to a cross upon a hill,
And He, before whose word the devils quailed,
Died like a common thief. He died—yet still
Where power and love contend for mastery,
Christ lives to win His deathless victory.

O God most righteous, and never more just than when Thou dost declare Thy terrible judgments upon Thy sinning people, forgive us by that mercy declared unto us by Thy Son on the cross. For we too have crucified Him. We, like the fickle mob, have called Him Lord with our lips and have refused to honor Him with our hearts and lives. We have sung hosannas to His name and have failed Him under testing. Forgive us, O God.

Then in Thy mercy deliver us from evil. Keep us ever mindful, in spite of the world's derision, that where destruction and death meet love and grace, it is Christ's way alone that conquers. Help us even in deepest darkness to wait for the glad morning of Thy victory over sin and death. Through Him who died for us and rose again. AMEN.

47

SIMON OF CYRENE

Daughters of Jerusalem, do not weep for me, but weep for yourselves and for your children.—Luke 23:28 (R.S.V.)

I walked that day out to the death-marked hill—
They call the place "the skull"—and saw Him bear
His cross until He fell. It was not fair,
I thought, to place it on Him. Strength and skill
Were mine from country toil. I bore it till
We came to Golgotha. I did not dare
To speak my grief; I only thought to spare
Him pain—His grateful look lives with me still.

And as we walked along, some women wept.
I could not censure them—my eyes were dim.
But know ye what He said? His words I've kept
Within my heart these years for love of Him:
"Weep not for me. Dark days await you too.
Forgive these men: they know not what they do."

Lord God our Father and the Father of our Lord Jesus Christ, our hearts are full at the thought of the grief He bore for us. Like Simon of Cyrene, we yearn to ease His pain, but we know we cannot, save by the full offering of our strength to Him. Like the women of Jerusalem, we weep at this dark tragedy when the purest of men died at the hands of sinners, but we know our tears are unavailing. One thing only can we do. Only as we walk the way of His cross can His mission be fulfilled in us. Help us, O Lord, to walk with Him all the way through the valley of the shadow to the glory of His risen presence, here and in eternity. AMEN.

GOOD FRIDAY

And when they came to the place which is called The Skull, there they crucified him, and the criminals, one on the right and one on the left. And Jesus said, "Father, forgive them; for they know not what they do."

—Luke 23:33-34 (R.S.V.)

We call it good—this day that marks the death
Of One who long ago was crucified.
He bled; He thirsted; writhed in pain. His breath
Came haltingly. "Forgive," He said, and died.

It was a felon's death. But thieves have hung
And good men too, on crosses many. Yet
No Friday marks the time. No hymns are sung;
No prayers are said. They sleep, and men forget.

Why call it good—that pregnant springtime day
When Jesus hung with thieves on Calvary?
He died for love of men. God led the way;
God saw my need; God suffered there for me.

This crucifixion day, let sin depart:
Lord, give me Easter gladness in my heart.

Eternal and all-loving God, who didst send Thy blessed Son to suffer and die for the saving of the world, look now in mercy and healing upon us, Thy sinful children. As He walked steadfastly to Jerusalem to suffer many things of dull and deceitful men, give us courage under testing. As He loved the humble and suffered reproach for the outcast, give us breadth of vision and depth of love. As He forgave His enemies, help us to live without enmity or rancor and to die at peace with Thee and with all men; through Him who died for us. AMEN.

THE MIRACLE

*Did not our hearts burn within us while he talked to us
on the road?*
                                        —Luke 24:32 (R.S.V.)

I know not how the miracle was wrought.
The story says the stone was rolled away;
That angels sat within as Mary sought
Her risen Lord; that linen grave cloths lay;
That Jesus stood there speaking words of cheer;
And walked with two along the Emmaus road;
That when eleven were gathered, sick with fear,
They felt His presence, saw the wounds He showed.

"How can it be?" I hear men say in doubt,
Like Thomas, who must see the nails' imprint.
I know not how these things could come about,
To read the mystery I have no hint:
But I have seen the Lord on Easter day,
My heart has burned within me in the way.

We rejoice, O God, with a joy too deep for words that Thou hast
sent Thy Son to dwell among us, to die in love for our redemption, to rise again to be with us forevermore. Today as in every
age He speaks to our fainting hearts, "Lo, I am with you always,
even unto the end of the world."

Before this miracle, O Lord, we bow in silence. Before it we
rise in joy to sing the glory of Thy triumph over death and sin.
In the power of this mystery of Thy love, let us walk and hold
communion, today and every day, with Christ our Saviour. In His
name we pray. AMEN.

50

SUNRISE

Then I saw a new heaven and a new earth. . . . And he who sat upon the throne said, "Behold, I make all things new." . . . And I saw no temple in the city, for its temple is the Lord God the Almighty and the Lamb.
—Rev. 21:1, 5, 22 (R.S.V.)

To John on Patmos' isle the vision came
Of jasper, amethyst, and chrysoprase,
Sardonyx, sapphire, multicolored flame
Of flashing jeweled walls. From out the haze
Of earthly things he saw a city rise
Foursquare, with pearls for gates and streets of gold,
Where tears should flow no more. Through opening skies
The seer beheld eternity unfold.

I saw a lovely lake at sunrise time.
Long fingers of the dawn brought flaming day.
It seemed as jewel-girded gold. Sublime,
With gates of pearl and jasper walls, it lay.
No temple needed John, nor I, for prayer:
A new day dawned, and God Himself there.

We thank Thee, Lord, that Thou hast made everything beautiful in its time. For the radiant splendor of a new day, as day unto day uttereth speech to tell of Thy glory, we give Thee gladsome praise. Help us to seize this day with eager souls and use it abundantly for Thee.

Hasten the day, O Lord, when Thy presence shall everywhere be manifest, and sin and strife shall be done away. Then shall Thy servants dwell with Thee in a new heaven and a new earth where sorrow and death shall be no more. We pray in the name of Him who said, "Behold, I make all things new." AMEN.

SUNSET

Holy, holy, holy, is the Lord of hosts: the whole earth is full of his glory.   —Isa. 6:3

I saw the new Jerusalem tonight.
The portals of the sky were opened wide;
The clouds were radiant with celestial light;
My lake gave back its answer, glorified.
Behold, there was a throne set high and clear;
An emerald rainbow circled it, all fair;
And four and twenty thrones, I think, were near,
For jasper, sardius, gold were everywhere.
Before the throne a sea of crystal glass,
And round about were creatures in the sky;
Across the sea a path of burnished brass,
And there, it seemed, angelic hosts drew nigh.
I thought I heard them singing as they trod,
Holy, holy, holy is Almighty God.

Lord of all being, throned afar, Thou hast spread Thy witness in beauty through all Thy world. The heavens declare Thy glory, and the firmament showeth Thy handiwork.

For the splendor of Thy divine artistry, for the majesty of earth and sky, for cloud-born messengers that speak of Thy holiness, we give Thee thanks. Before Thee we bow. Our lips are hushed. Our hearts are filled with Thy glory. AMEN.

NIGHTFALL BY A LAKE

He leadeth me beside the still waters. He restoreth my soul.
 —Ps. 23:2-3

Sparkling wavelets flashing;
Playful fishes splashing;
Waves of limpid blue;
Glint of every hue;
Flaming sunset glory
Over mountains hoary;
Heaven all aglow;
Earth asleep below.

Iridescent sheen;
Scent of evergreen;
Merry crickets singing;
Children's voices ringing;
Swish of moving oar;
Lights along the shore;
Music from afar;
Twinkling evening star.

Fretful strivings cease
In God's eternal peace.

We thank Thee, Lord, that Thou hast made Thy world so fair. Its beauty and peace, its grandeur and glory, speak to us of Thee. By the changing seasons; playful living things; soft skies and flaming sunsets; mountains and valleys; fertile fields and green trees; oceans, rivers, lakes, and much else that Thou hast spread with prodigal hand, we are drawn to Thee.

As these lead us into Thy holy presence, let our hearts be attuned to speak with Thee in rich communion. Give us, as Thou seest our need requires, rest for our bodies and peace for our souls. AMEN.

THE STARRY HEAVENS AND THE MORAL LAW

For thou hast made him but little lower than God,
And crownest him with glory and honor.
> —Ps. 8:5 (A.S.V.)

"How excellent Thy name in all the earth,
Jehovah God!" the Psalmist cried. He saw
The jeweled sky, the moon and stars, the birth
Of God-created things, and bowed in awe.
He could but kneel before such majesty,
Bereft of pride, as finite humans must;
Too great a thing it seemed, for God to be
Akin to man, and lift him from the dust.

Again he looked: he saw the holy God,
And then—O miracle!—it seemed he stood
Only a step below—no human clod,
But *man!* man glorified, divine, wise, good!
He pondered long how God and man were kin,
And glimpsed the bond—the moral law within.

We thank Thee, O God, for the majestic beauty of the earth and sky, for Thy bountiful provision for warmth and light to nourish us by day and shining radiance to kindle our souls by night. Before the magnificent distances and infinite orderliness of the heavens we bow in awe, and cry out with the psalmist of old, "O Lord, our Lord, how excellent is thy name in all the earth!"

Yet his question too is ours. How canst Thou be mindful of man in so vast a universe? We rejoice, O God, that Thou hast not left us without an answer. For our human kind, made in Thine own image, we give Thee grateful praise. Sinners though we be, Thou hast made us creatures of infinite worth in Thy sight. Assured that all are beloved and honored of Thee, we would love and honor all men. Direct us, Lord, as we seek to view our brothers through Thy eyes and do to them as Thou wouldst have us do. AMEN.

THE PEACE OF GOD

In his hand are the deep places of the earth: the strength of the hills is his also.
                                                              —Ps. 95:4

I will lift up mine eyes unto the hills,
The everlasting mountains of the Lord,
And feel within me that great calm that stills
Unrest, the peace that holy things afford.

Snow-crowned in beauty, chaste and strong they stand,
Unmoved by restive turmoil of the earth;
They speak of long eternities and grand
Wherein their Maker brings His will to birth.

And so, O little man, why hurry so?
And let your life be fevered with alarms?
God has great patience; it takes time to grow;
Trust Him, and like the hills lean on His arms.
You mountain peaks, so calm, serene, and strong,
You and my questing soul to God belong.

We rejoice, O God, in Thy mountains. Before the majesty of the everlasting hills our souls are humbled, lifted up, made strong. Through them Thou dost speak to still our fretfulness and subdue our haste. Through them Thou dost speak to us of beauty, strength, and peace.

We know, O Lord, that before the mountains were brought forth, or ever Thou hadst formed the earth and the world, even from everlasting to everlasting, Thou art God. In this knowledge we would rest, and wait for Thee to move in Thine own chosen ways. AMEN.

VIGIL

Awake, thou that sleepest.   —Eph. 5:14 (A.S.V.)

In peace I will both lie down and sleep;
  for thou alone, O Lord, makest me dwell in safety.
                          —Ps. 4:8 (R.S.V.)

Matins—
Blue of flashing sapphire on a lake,
Blue of tinted azure in the skies,
Blue that melts with green and gold and rose
To make of earth celestial harmonies.

Compline—
Gray of mist-filled air and leaden clouds,
Gray of barren fields and sleeping streams,
Gray of weathered barns and leaf-stript trees
That makes of earth a couch for Lethean dreams.

And blue and gray their vigil keep—
In blue I wake, in gray I sleep.

We thank Thee, O Lord, for glad awakenings within Thy world and within our hearts. For the beauty that stirs our souls awake and the greater radiance of Thy living presence, we praise and bless Thee. We would serve Thee with gladness and come into Thy presence with singing.

For the rhythm of rest in nature and within ourselves we would praise and bless Thee too. In peace we would lie down and sleep, for Thy arms surround and Thy love enfolds us. Lighten our darkness, we beseech Thee, O Lord; and by Thy great mercy defend us from all perils and dangers of the night, for the love of Thy only Son, our Saviour, Jesus Christ. AMEN.

SILENCES

Keep silence before me, O islands; and let the people renew their strength.
                                              —Isa. 41:1

Three silences were eloquent,
They woke my spirit, dull and spent—

The silence of a lake at night,
God spoke to me through flashing bands of light.

The silence of a lonely hill,
Birds twittered softly and all else was still.

The silence of a sleeping child,
He gently stirred, yawned drowsily, and smiled.

We rejoice, O God, in the silences that speak to us of Thee. Amid the hurry and confusion of our busy lives, so full of duties and demands that jostle and press upon us, we would be still and know that Thou art God. Amid the great serenities of Thy world we would listen to hear Thee speak. In the presence of fair human souls, whether in infancy fresh from Thy hand or in maturity made rich from fellowship with Thee, we would be still and know that Thou art not far away.

Quiet, O God, the tumult of our hearts, and let our lips and our minds be silent before Thee. So by Thy grace shall our strength be renewed. Amen.

THE SIGNATURE OF GOD

O Lord, how manifold are thy works!
In wisdom hast thou made them all;
the earth is full of thy creatures.
—Ps. 104:24 (R.S.V.)

In sparkling radiance of earth and sky,
In quiet hills where cattle graze, content,
In mountain fastness, verdure-walled and high,
In these are writ a glory that was lent.

The flashing loveliness of sun-lit sea,
The graceful birds that skim its foam-flecked breast,
Each gladsome bough and blossom, winter-free,
Speak to my soul of rapture and of rest.

Thou madest, Lord, Thy world to be so fair
Which men in folly mar with strife and fear;
But open now my eyes and let me dare
Believe Thy hand is sure, Thy heart is near.

For when such beauty speaks and bids me pray,
I know the Light of Life shines on our way.

Glory be to Thee, O Lord! For earth and sky, mountains and seas, birds and flowers, all the many lovely things of Thy world, we bless and praise Thee! Manifold are Thy works; in wisdom hast Thou made them all; the earth is full of the riches of Thy creation.

Let us never, O Lord, be dull to this beauty so freely given or to the goodness of Thy handiwork. As men of old in awe before the glory of Thy creation declared, "And God saw that it was good," so may we ever believe and witness, even in darkest days. To Thee we pledge joyous, grateful, trusting hearts. AMEN.

SPRING'S HERE!

For, lo, the winter is past, the rain is over and gone. The flowers appear on the earth; the time of the singing of birds is come. —Song of Solomon 2:11-12

The dull drab winter days are past.
The sleeping buds, imprisoned fast
Within tree-tips that looked like death,
Are breathing forth their warm sweet breath.
The grassy carpet on each hill,
Forsythia and daffodil,
Are bursting into greens and golds
To sing the cheer all Nature holds.
The crocuses lift up their heads
To nod to gladsome tulip beds;
The robins chirp a merry song
To urge the floral dance along.
The spring's bright banner is unfurled:
Look up, my soul, sing with the world!

We thank Thee, Lord of all, for the changing seasons, which in many moods speak eloquently of Thy gladness in creation. Thou who hast made our world so beautiful, we know Thou dost rejoice in Thy handiwork and call us with glad hearts to rejoice with Thee.

Let the new life that courses through all Nature stir within us, Lord. Give us fresh vigor not only to rejoice with Thee but to labor for Thee. And may the new life that we see in all growing things speak to us of newness of life beyond our wintry snows, in Thine eternal kingdom. Through Christ our Lord. AMEN.

THE WATERS OF THE RESTING PLACE

*He maketh me to lie down in green pastures: he leadeth
me beside the still waters.* —Ps. 23:2

> He leads me to the waters of the resting place
>   And there restores my soul.
> Amid the whispering poplars by a lovely lake
>   He makes my spirit whole.
>
> In friendly presence tables are spread bounteously;
>   In pastures green I lie;
> The weariness of toil, the cares, the fears, depart;
>   I know that God is nigh.

O God in whom we live and move and have our being, we
rejoice that at all times Thy world proclaims Thy invigorating
strength and Thy gracious care. Especially do we praise Thee
now for the kindly warmth of summer sunshine, for the glory
of green grass and many-colored flowers, for rustling trees and
sparkling waters. Let these speak to us, O God, to restore our
souls.

We know, our Father, that Thou dost intend these good gifts
for all and would have none of Thy children denied them. Enlarge
our compassion and our vision, and help us so to order our
world that all may share in these gifts which Thou dost so freely
bestow.

Take not Thy Holy Spirit from us, O Lord, but restore unto
us the joy of Thy salvation. AMEN.

AUTUMN HILLS

I lift up my eyes to the hills.
From whence does my help come?
My help comes from the Lord,
Who made heaven and earth.
        —Ps. 121:1-2 (R.S.V.)

"I will lift up mine eyes unto the hills,
From whence there cometh strength as from our God,"
So sang the Psalmist as of old he trod
Judea's rugged slopes, and found in rills
And waterfalls, in mountain crags, in trills
Of birds, in flaming trees, in very clod,
The splendor and the majesty of God,
Who fashions all in age-long ceaseless mills.

Today I walked and lifted up my eyes
To other hills, to other mountain heights
Aglow with saffron radiance and calm
With autumn's gentle potency, to skies
Serene. I saw a world that strength invites,
And in my soul, unvoiced, there stirred a psalm.

We thank Thee, Maker of heaven and earth, for the gracious and tender beauty of the autumn—for trees aflame with color, for fields laden with the harvest, for soft skies and gentle sunshine. And we would look up to the hills that speak to us of Thy everlasting strength, and draw our strength from Thine.

Give us, O Lord, the beauty of soul to which Thy world, so radiant with beauty, calls us. Endue us with the courage and the patience of which Thou dost remind us by the calm steadfastness of Thy mountains. Guard us from fretfulness and unwonted haste, as these tell us that Thou dost never hasten, and grant the strength we need to labor for Thee from day to day. Through Christ our Lord. AMEN.

INVICTA

Thou hast fixed all the bounds of the earth;
thou hast made summer and winter.
—Ps. 74:17 (R.S.V.)

I went to walk at winter twilight time
And saw the world alive with strength sublime:
White birches shorn of leaves but not of grace,
Their branches meeting in a mad embrace,
Their trunks agleam against the stone wall's gray—
And this as void of elegance as they,
But like them proudly sure of spring's return
And with it verdure, incense from the urn
That Nature's priests keep burning endlessly.

I saw an old gray barn that once, as free
As youth at twenty-one, had stood and scoffed
The gales. Chill winds now whistle through its loft;
It leans to leeward, not quite firm, and yet
Uncowed, it smiles at Time and pays its debt.

Against the pearl-white sky, gray clouds looked old—
But touched with sunset glow, their ashen cold
Was lit with radiant life; for power and peace
Fail not when snowflakes fall and bird-songs cease.

When I walked abroad at winter twilight time,
I saw the whited earth all cleansed of grime;
I saw the roving vines that, restless, creep
Their way through summer days, now calmly sleep.
I saw the virile earth, the dauntless sky,
Meet winter, bow, and then refuse to die:
For every snow-crowned stone, each rugged tree
Proclaimed its gospel of serenity.

Help us, good Lord, to learn the lessons Thou dost teach us in
all Thy creation; and give us faith to wait through the winter of
our hopes till the springtime comes again. AMEN.

CHRISTMAS CAROL

*And suddenly there was with the angel a multitude of
the heavenly host praising God, and saying, Glory to God
in the highest, and on earth peace, good will toward men.*

—Luke 2:13

A heavenly host sang in the night
　　To tell the glorious birth
Of One who came to rule men's hearts,
　　To bring good news to earth.
Far down the echoing halls of time
　　We hear the angels sing.
"Glory to God and on earth peace"—
　　Their clear hosannas ring.

Glad voices still lift up the song
　　Across the storm-swept years:
Yet still men hate and strive for gold
　　And hearts are sick with fears.
"Joy to the world," the anthem rings;
　　But God must weep instead.
Do nations hail the Prince of Peace
　　When men cry out for bread?

Not yet has Bethlehem's holy babe
　　Been born in states and marts.
God cannot joy until He dwells
　　In human minds and hearts.
This Christmastide when carols ring
　　To hail the Christ Child's birth,
May He come in to rule in love,
　　May Peace be born on earth.

Grant, O God, this longing of our hearts and the desire of all the
nations. May peace be born on earth, that the night of war may
be done away and the glad morning come. AMEN.

63

CHRISTMAS EVE

But Mary kept all these things, pondering them in her heart. —Luke 2:20 (R.S.V.)

For crisp, clear splendor of a winter night,
For snow and stars, and heaven's immensity,
For glory of the Lord in radiant light,
    For these I thank Thee.

For sleeping field, and sturdy snow-clad fir
That lifts its laden arms as if each tree
Would bring its gift of frankincense and myrrh,
    For these I thank Thee.

For stables snug, and warmth for man and beast,
For fellowship with folk of low degree,
For time-tried lore of wise men from the East,
    For these I thank Thee.

For each new Mary, and the wondrous tale
Announcing her young child's high destiny
Till pondering, she makes his life her Grail,
    For these I thank Thee.

We thank Thee, Lord, for the high heritage of joyous song, of kindliness and cheer, of knowledge of heavenly Presence among earth's humble ones, that Christmas brings again. May we like the shepherds of old go in haste to find the babe of Bethlehem and tell His wondrous story, and like the wise men come to lay before Him our best gifts.

As Mary kept all these things, pondering them in her heart, let our hearts be filled with the marvel and mystery of Thy coming for our redemption. Help us never to forget that Thou hast come to dwell among us—that Thou art here! So let our prayer of Christmas time be the desire of every heart through all the days,

O come to my heart, Lord Jesus,
There is room in my heart for Thee.

AMEN.

A CHRISTMAS LULLABY

*To you is born this day in the city of David a Savior,
who is Christ the Lord.* —Luke 2:11 (R.S.V.)

> Sleep, little Jesus, sleep.
> May holy angels keep
> You safe through all the night.
> So close your eyes so bright,
> Sleep, little Jesus, sleep.
>
> Sleep, little Jesus child,
> So sweet and undefiled,
> You came from heaven above
> To bring all children love.
> Sleep, little Jesus child.
>
> Sleep, little Jesus boy;
> The humble shout their joy,
> The wise come from afar,
> To worship where you are.
> Sleep, little Jesus boy.
>
> Sleep, little Jesus, sleep.
> May God your spirit keep;
> Then wake to joy and mirth,
> Best gift of God to earth!
> Sleep, little Jesus, sleep.

Our blessed Lord, who in love didst come to earth in the holy child of Bethlehem, come dwell with us tonight.

Make tender our souls to children everywhere, that in them too Thy image may shine brightly. Guard and guide the mothers of every land, that with souls lighted by Thee they may rear their little ones to lives of health and goodness and knowledge of Thee. Enlarge now our compassion, that none may suffer in hunger and want or be lacking in the love that Jesus came to bring.

May the gladness and good cheer of Christmas go with us all till this season comes again. Through Him who slept in a manger. AMEN.

65

ADESTE FIDELES

Fear not; for, behold, I bring you good tidings of great joy, which shall be to all people. —Luke 2:10

Gnarled old faces, crippled limbs,
Men at a poor farm singing hymns.

Laeti triumphantes, the carols ring:
But "the old rugged cross" is what these sing.
. . . .
Virginal faces unseared by life,
Naught know these of rigor and strife.

Joyous, triumphant, their paeans rise—
But depths of days must make them wise.
. . . .
Shepherds and Magi, led by one light,
Met to adore Him on that holy night.

Old men and maidens, singing for joy,
Joy in their homage to Bethlehem's boy.

O God of Jesus, who dost enfold in Thy loving heart and keep with Thy gracious care all manner of men, we praise and bless Thee for our greatest gift, our Saviour Christ. For His glorious birth amid humble folk when the heavenly chorus sang of peace on earth, for His words of life and light and His blessed ministry, for His death on a cross for our redemption, we give Thee thanks beyond the power of human words to speak.

In common joyous praise to Thee and in contemplation of the mystery of Thy love that has sent us such a Saviour, let all earthly differences be leveled, all human walls cast down. Let our worship with one voice ring true within a fellowship of hearts. So shall Thy name be honored and Thy Son's work be done. In His name we pray. AMEN.

TO THE NEW YEAR

One generation goeth, and another generation cometh;
but the earth abideth for ever. —Eccl. 1:4 (A.S.V.)

In cold of crunching snow and frozen breath
The old year falls asleep and ends its day.
In warmth of tingling blood that knows no death
The new takes up the course and speeds away.
Run well the race, young life, and know no fear!
New goals shall crown the circuit of the year!

We thank Thee, O God, for time and change, which give variety and zest to our passing lives. We thank Thee for the great stabilities that hold us firm within the changing seasons and the moving years.

We lay before Thee the year that is past, full of failures and shortcomings which we confess in shame before Thee, but also gladdened by little successes and made bright with high moments of happiness. Weave this year as Thou canst into the making of Thy kingdom.

Go with us, Lord, into the year that lies before us. Help us to face its unseen possibilities bravely and hopefully. Be Thou our Companion, our Guide, our strong Defense when sin or sorrow confronts us. Enlarge our horizons; give us new goals; quicken us daily to be more faithful servants of Thine. Then when we have done the best we can, help us in patience and trust to leave the issue with Thee. Through Christ our Lord. AMEN.

A LENTEN MEDITATION

*Do not lay up for yourselves treasures on earth, . . . but
lay up for yourselves treasures in heaven. . . . For where
your treasure is, there will your heart be also.*
—Matt. 6:19-21 (R.S.V.)

Two thousand years ago there died upon a cross
A dark-haired, clear-eyed youth of thirty-three.
He was a Jew. A workman's son was he,
Of stalwart, supple build—and he could toss
A timber in his father's shop across
The bench with muscle firm, or fell a tree,
Or swing a child aloft to shouts of glee.
But, spent, he sank one day beneath his cross.
One of Cyrene bore it to the hill
And there he died in shame between two thieves—
This Jew who bade men turn from quest of pelf.
And why? He tried to do His Father's will,
To do it in a world that yet perceives
The greatness of His way, and follows self.

Our eternal and all-wise God, who hast not called us to the getting
of earthly wealth but to the laying up of treasure in heaven,
help us to think Thy thoughts and to walk in Thy ways. We thank
Thee for the example of Thy blessed Son, who, taking the form
of a servant and working with men in the humble tasks of life,
still wrought eternally for Thee. Through Him who was obedient
unto death, even the death of the cross, we pledge our obedience
to Thee.

Help us, O Lord, to look upon all of life as Thy holy calling.
Whether in our work, our play, our fellowship with others, or
our worship of Thee, we would seek to gather true riches. Then
at the last wilt Thou take us to Thy nearer presence, there to
rejoice with Thee in the heavenly treasure Thou hast in store for
us. Through Christ our Lord. AMEN.

FOR GOD SO LOVED THE WORLD

*For God so loved the world that he gave his only Son,
that whoever believes in him should not perish but have
eternal life.* —John 3:16 (R.S.V.)

"For God so loved the world He gave His Son
That all believing on Him might have life."
The resurrection morn, God's victory won,
Gleams clear above the carnage and the strife
To say to souls distraught and wracked with pain,
To multitudes that watch in darkest night:
"Think not, O world, the Lord Christ died in vain.
He lives to save, to lift men to the light."

For God so loved the world He gave His Son
To bring eternity to death-bound earth,
To win the souls of men to dwell as one
In peace and fellowship, good will and mirth.
This day let Christ be risen in my heart,
That I may see Thee, Father, as Thou art.

Almighty God our Saviour, before the gift of Thine own Son
for our salvation our lips are mute with joy and thanksgiving.
We have erred and strayed from Thy ways like lost sheep. We
have offended against Thy holy laws. Yet in love Thou didst
send Thy Son for our redemption; in mercy Thou dost forgive
and receive us to Thyself.

Help us, Lord, to hold fast our confession. Make us steadfast
to draw near with confidence to Thy throne of grace, that we
may receive mercy and find grace to help us in time of need.

This we would do in glad rejoicing that Christ lived and died
for us and rose victorious over sin and death. In the name of
Him who is ever the Way, the Truth, and the Life we pray. AMEN.

AFTER EASTER

Lo, I am with you always, even unto the end of the world.
　　　　　　　　　　　—Matt. 28:20 (A.S.V.)

On Easter day my heart is lifted high
With gladsome praises to the Lord of life.
The hallelujahs ring: the heavens are rife
With song and story. He who could defy
The powers of death has risen again—is nigh
To say, "Fear not . . . Men, put away your strife,
I am the resurrection and the life."
All earth seems joyous, and we need not die!

The vision fades; the Easter joy is past;
Again in dull drab paths our lot is cast.
The heavens no longer sing. The war clouds lower.
O Lord, where art Thou in Thy risen power?
The calm voice speaks—it answers all I ask,
"I am beside you in the daily task."

We would praise Thee, O God, with the glad hallelujahs of
Easter. In flowers that speak of Thy purity and our joy, in anthems
that ring out to tell the wondrous story, in words of holy Scripture
heard a thousand times yet ever new, we come to lay before Thee
our tribute of rejoicing.

The days pass and our hearts grow dull. Duties press upon us,
and anxieties and sorrows multiply. We long for release, and our
hearts cry out, "How long, O Lord, how long?"

Be with us, O God, every day and all the way. Keep our hearts
and our minds in Christ Jesus. Give us that steadfast love that
bears all things, believes all things, hopes all things, endures
all things. So shall our ordered lives sing praise to Thee, not
with anthems of rejoicing, but with that greater peace that passes
all understanding. Through Christ our Lord. AMEN.

UPON BEGINNING A VACATION

In returning and rest you shall be saved;
in quietness and in trust shall be your strength.
—Isa. 30:15 (R.S.V.)

Give us, O Lord, Thy quietness and calm;
In stillness we would find Thy healing balm.

Now must we go apart and rest awhile,
For Thou didst bid us, Lord, to love Thee—
To love Thee not alone with mind and soul and heart,
But love Thee, too, with all our strength.
And when the body faints, the soul grows dull,
Then have we sinned against ourselves and Thee,
If, pausing not, we gather not anew
The firmer texture of the mind and heart,
The strength of tissue and of nerve,
That come from rest in Thee
And in the mothering bosom of Thy world.

And so, O Lord, we give our bodies up
Into Thy keeping. Guard them secure;
Take them as incense offered unto Thee,
And when Thine altar fires have burned away the dross,
Restore them strong enough to bear Thy cross.

We thank Thee, O God, for the great rhythms of life—for summer and winter, for cold and warmth, for day and night, for waking and sleeping, for work and rest. Help us to labor zealously, and whatsoever our hands find to do, to do it with our might. Guard us from anxious fretfulness, and keep us ever mindful that the issues of our labor are not in our hands alone, but in Thine. Then help us to turn again from our wonted toil to refreshment and rest. So shall we gather strength for the new day and for the new year that in Thy good providence lies before us.

In Thee, O God, is our quietness and our trust. In Thee we would rest and be strong. AMEN.

THANKSGIVING

Bless the Lord, O my soul: and all that is within me,
bless his holy name. —Ps. 103:1

Father all bountiful,
    Thee we adore,
Filling our treasure house
    Out of Thy store.
By Thee our years are blest;
    By Thee we live.
Grateful, we take from Thee
    All Thou dost give.

Though darkness shrouds the lands,
    Still shines Thy light.
Mercies that flow from Thee
    Gladden our night.
Blessings of home and kin,
    Friendship and health,
Come from Thy gracious hand
    In boundless wealth.

Father who givest all,
    To Thee we bring
Tribute of grateful hearts;
    Thy praises sing.
Help us to use Thy gifts
    To spread Thy peace;
Give us Thy Spirit, Lord,
    Our love increase.

Thou Giver of all good gifts, accept with our lives, now rededicated to Thee, our tribute of grateful praise. In Thee we trust; be Thou our strength. AMEN.

HOLY FLAME

*And I heard the voice of the Lord, saying, Whom shall
I send, and who will go for us? Then I said, Here am I;
send me.* —Isa. 6:8 (A.S.V.)

Isaiah mourned the passing of the king,
And to the temple came to muse and pray.
Dark was the kingdom's future on that day,
Beset with greed and every evil thing.
No spokesman of the Lord was there to sting
The conscience of the mob, or lead the way
To gallant victories in Jehovah's fray
With sin and strife, with self and suffering.

God gave Isaiah then the vision high;
His unclean lips were purged with sacred fire;
Out of the smoke a Voice in challenge came;
Unhesitant, he answered, Here am I.
Again the days are dark, the outlook dire;
Lord, touch Thy prophets now with holy flame.

We thank Thee, O God, for prophets of every age who have
caught a vision of Thy truth and have dared to call men to the
doing of Thy will. Kindle anew, we pray, a burning zeal for
Thy holy goodness.

Give Thy Church a new urgency before the heavy demands
and high opportunities of this day. Endue it with a fresh awareness of its power in Thee. May it give comfort to the sorrowing,
strength to the burdened, peace of soul to the anxious and the
oppressed. Let its ministers speak boldly Thy word of judgment
upon the sins of our time and proclaim the good news of Thy
salvation.

Redeem Thy Church, O God, and use it for the redemption
of a stricken world. In Thy light let us see light, that the gospel
of Christ may shine upon a world that sits in darkness and the
shadow of death. In His name we pray. AMEN.

INASMUCH—

Inasmuch as ye have done it unto one of the least of these my brethren, ye have done it unto me.—Matt. 25:40

Inasmuch . . . The words cut through my heart.
Oft have I heard them, read them, passed them by
To go about my tasks and do my part
In the day's work. But now men starve and die!
Secure I dwell. Enough have I to eat
And wear. I saw no deadly firebrand fall
To shatter all I had in dire defeat.
I live in comfort; they beneath a pall.
I see them—but Another I behold,
Bleeding, thorn-crowned, dying on a cross.
If I feed not the hungry, warm the cold,
Visit the sick and lonely in their loss,
Inasmuch . . . as I did it not for men,
Then Thee, O Christ, I crucify again.

O God our Father, we give Thee thanks for Thy great bounty. Thou hast placed us in a world that is abundant in goods for our daily bread and rich with all manner of gifts. Within it Thou hast set us as Thy stewards to work with Thee and to share Thy gifts with all the sons of men.

Thou hast given us much; in shame we confess the littleness of our return. We have sought our own ease and comfort. We have wasted Thy gifts while others of Thy sons have suffered grievously in hunger and want. Forgive us, O Lord, and make us more faithful stewards.

We pray, O God, for our brethren and Christ's. Wherever war, or hunger, or poverty, or disease, or racial prejudice, or man's inhumanity has closed the doors to health and happiness, help us to open them. Let all that we have be dedicated to Thee for the increase of love and the good life among all men. In Christ's name. AMEN.

74

MARCHING MEN

*They shall beat their swords into plowshares, and their
spears into pruning-hooks; nation shall not lift up sword
against nation, neither shall they learn war any more.*
—Isa. 2:4 (A.S.V.)

I hear the sound of marching men.
Across the years with measured tread
They march—the living and the dead.

I hear the sound of marching men.
The shouts of victory I hear
While men are moaning—dying—near.

I hear the sound of marching men.
I thought I heard the song of peace;
Yet on they march. Will marching cease?

I hear the sound of marching men.
They march to die: they march to kill.
I hear them marching, marching still . . .

We pray Thee, O God, that war may soon perish from the earth.
Too long has it held men chained to destruction and death. Too
feeble has been our faith that a better way is possible.

We would pray for peace, not lightly with our lips, but earn-
estly with our lives. Help us to overcome evil with good in the
daily relations of our lives, that reconciling love may do its healing work beginning where we are. Help us to see all men as our
brothers, and to pray in pity for those who follow not Thy way.
Wherever strife or enmity, hatred or fear is found, there let our
voices and our deeds and the outreach of our hearts speak forth
for justice and good will. Take the courage and self-giving of
marching men and of those who for conscience' sake refuse to
kill, and in Thine infinite wisdom use this sacrifice for the advancement of Thy kingdom of righteousness and peace. In the
name of the Prince of Peace. AMEN.

GOD MADE EARTH FAIR

He has made everything beautiful in its time. . . . I know
. . . also that it is God's gift to man that every one should eat
and drink and take pleasure in all his toil.
　　　　　　　　　　　　　　—Eccl. 3:11-13 (R.S.V.)

The world is full of madness and of din:
The dogs of war, unleashed, bay at the moon.
Is it some wild and frolicsome buffoon—
Some world dementia, battening on sin—
That leers at truth and with unholy grin
Dances on human souls? A mournful loon
Makes dirgelike music for the sport. How soon
Will end this frenzy, snaring wise men in?

God made earth fair that man might live in love.
The air is soft: the leaves are gently stirring:
The blue waves sing a little psalm of peace:
The clouds are billowy white and still above,
Not made for bombing aircraft's deadly purring.
When shall this mindless, mad perversion cease?

We thank Thee, O God, for the beauty of the earth and for the
good things by which our lives have been made rich. In shame
we confess that we grievously have marred Thy handiwork. The
world Thou madest fair for all the sons of men has become a
place of darkness and death, of fear and suspicion and hate.
Forgive us, O Lord, this sin for which by our indifference or our
evil deeds we all stand condemned.

We pray Thee, O God, for those who are in great suffering.
Grant Thy presence to the anxious, the bereaved, the uprooted,
the homeless, the hungry, the wounded, the dying, the desolate,
those many millions who because of war sit in darkness and the
shadow of death. Let Thy light shine upon them, and deliver
them. And give peace in our time, O Lord, for Thou only makest
us to dwell in safety. AMEN.

DAY OF JUDGMENT

Is it nothing to you, all you who pass by?
—Lam. 1:12 (R.S.V.)

Starvation stalks. The ghosts of dead men laid,
We fondly dreamed that peace once more might reign,
And swords give way to plowshares while earth's frayed
And tattered remnants were made whole again.

Now spectral hunger forays everywhere,
Save in this land where opulence is rife.
The faces of the living dead declare
That God is mocked, Mars victor in the strife.

Did Christ not die to save us from our sin?
Do we not care that these His brethren die?
Shall we, as Christless, wall our plenty in?
Is it nothing to us, all we that pass by?

Then shall the God of judgment sound our knell
And earth be plunged again in nether hell.

O God, in whose will is our peace, we rejoice that in Christ our Lord Thou hast shown us the way out of darkness. Help us to find and follow this way, that there may be peace on earth, good will among men.

We have sinned against Thee and our brothers, Thy sons. We merit Thy righteous judgment. By our greed of gain and pride of race, by our selfish complacency and indifference to wrong, by our hoarding to ourselves what Thou hast entrusted to us, and by the littleness of our love toward those of other nations, we have helped to bring war upon the world. Forgive us, and cleanse us of the tempers that make for strife.

Help us, O Lord, not to be overcome by evil but to overcome evil with good. In Christ's name. AMEN.

THE TWILIGHT IS TURNED INTO TREMBLING

The twilight I longed for
has been turned for me into trembling.
—Isa. 21:4 (R.S.V.)

The twilight is turned into trembling,
The watchers see horsemen abreast,
The day is filled with confusion,
The night yieldeth dark, but not rest.

A voice crieth out of the darkness,
"O watchman, what of the night?"
From the tower the oracle soundeth,
"Inquire ye, turn to the light!"

Abroad are destruction and weeping,
In revels men lightly rejoice;
But the twilight is turned into trembling,
For the signs of the times are His voice.

We thank Thee, our Father, for Thy steadfast love and for the knowledge that even in darkest days Thou art our refuge and strength, a very present help in trouble.

In this time of tragedy and destiny be with those in places of danger, and if it be possible, bring them in safety to their homes. Give them strength and courage, and help them to know that whether in life or in death, nothing can sever them from Thy love and care.

Be with those whose hearts are anxious for those they love. Give them the assurance that nothing can pluck them out of the Father's hand and that in Thy good keeping all is well.

Grant Thy Spirit to those whom the world calls our enemies, and lead them with ourselves from darkness to light.

Help us all to yield ourselves to Thy service for the bringing of peace with justice upon earth. Through the dark ways of these times let Thy Kingdom come and Thy will be done. AMEN.

PROMETHEUS

Though the fig tree do not blossom,
nor fruit be on the vines,
the produce of the olive fail
and the fields yield no food,
the flock be cut off from the fold
and there be no herd in the stalls,
yet I will rejoice in the Lord,
I will joy in the God of my salvation.
—Hab. 3:17-18 (R.S.V.)

I would give thanks today. But all around
I see the plight of those whom Circumstance
Has caught within its cutting chains and bound
Prometheus-like, upon the mount of Chance.
So planless, mad, chaotic seem these things—
Strong men brought low, and spirits sick with fear,
As if some giant vulture's gleaming wings
Were circling man and what he holds most dear.

I can give thanks today. For spirits high,
Promethean, refuse to bend the knee
To Circumstance—when chains cut deep, defy
Their power to bind a soul forever free.
Such folk I know. Their courage lights the way.
For these, O God, I give Thee thanks today.

O God our Father, who art ever near and never nearer than
when all earthly supports fail, grant us a clear awareness of Thy
presence. We bless Thee for the example of those valiant souls
who in war, and persecution, and hunger, and want, and peril,
and pain, and the loss of all things save their faith in Thee, have
yet trusted Thee unto death.

Give us, O Lord, courage in our darkness, light upon our duties,
and patience to wait for better days. But above all, grant us to
know that the eternal God is our dwelling place and underneath
are the everlasting arms. Through Christ our Lord. AMEN.

TO A GREAT SOUL, NOW DEPARTED

*I am the resurrection and the life; he who believes in me,
though he die, yet shall he live.*—John 11:25 (R.S.V.)

Take Thou the man he was,
And is, and shall be in Thy heavenly home—
Take him to Thy nearer presence, Lord,
As we lift up our hearts
To praise Thee for the gift
Of this great gentle, strong, and loving soul.

To know him was to know Thee too—
To find good cheer within the common way,
To live alert and challenged to be strong,
To love, to serve, to find each soul Thy kin.
Because he dwelt with men, men dwelt with Thee.

And though our eyes shall now no more behold
The smiling goodness of his kindly face,
His gentle strength, invigorating grace,
We know that in Thy world—
Within Thy treasury of priceless goods—
He lives!

He lives—
Thy friend, O Lord, and ours—
He lived with us to drive the dark away:
He lives with Thee in endless, fairer day.

Eternal Father, whose love is everlasting, whose mercy endureth
forever, comfort now with Thy living presence those who mourn
the loss of those they love. Help us, who remember before Thee
those whom we no longer see, to live with stronger faith and
brighter radiance because they have touched our lives. Into Thy
hands we commend their spirits, assured that in Thy heavenly
realm there is joy and peace. AMEN.

THE SHEPHERD OF THE FLOCK

And his gifts were that some should be apostles, some prophets, some evangelists, some pastors and teachers, for the equipment of the saints, for the work of ministry, for building up the body of Christ.

—Eph. 4:11-12 (R.S.V.)

With kindly heart and unpretending ways
He moves among his flock and brings good cheer.
His smile, his listening love, casts out the fear
Of those on whom the blight of worry lays
Its poisoning touch. He speaks a word of praise
To each who labors in the fold. To hear
His friendly greeting is to feel a clear,
Fine radiance that lives above the maze.
One may not call him eloquent, and yet
The wisdom that he speaks in homely terms
Shows converse with a Power that dwells above.
To hear him is to worship God and let
Base thought depart. Such shepherding confirms
His people's faith and hope, and makes them love.

O God, we thank Thee for the Church and for the calling of some to be its ministers. For those pastors who have blessed our lives we give Thee grateful praise.

Give Thy servants, Lord, wisdom and strength for the great tasks of our day. Endue Thy ministers with righteousness. May they be taught of Thee to give comfort to the sorrowing, strength to the burdened. Let their faith be undimmed, that they may be clear witnesses to Thy truth. Let their courage be high, that they may proclaim boldly Thy righteous judgments. Let their love be strong, that they may be good ministers of Thy mercy and grace.

Grant Thy presence, Lord, to all who are members of the body of Christ, and build us up in Thy service. Help us each to give Thee the best we have. In Christ's name. AMEN.

THE BUILDER

*Do your best to present yourself to God as one approved,
a workman who has no need to be ashamed, rightly handling
the word of truth.* —II Tim. 2:15 (R.S.V.)

A master builder in the Lord's domain,
He sets each stone in place with neat precision.
Strong is his hand. Where giant evils reign
He lifts his arm to strike with firm decision;
Where life meets life in intricate design
His touch is delicate, his eye sees true.
So stone on stone he builds—and line on line—
A living structure old yet ever new.

If you should ask from whence he has this gift—
This art to fashion life in strength and grace,
It lies not in his craft or might. To lift
The stone the workman humbly gives God place,
And from His Spirit comes the power sublime
To build God's house eternally in time.

We rejoice, O God, that Thou hast given to some to be apostles,
some prophets, some evangelists, some pastors and teachers. To
some Thou hast given to be all of these for the perfecting of human
lives, for the work of ministering, for the building up of the body
of Christ.

For those who with one talent or with ten have given themselves to Thee in humble devotion and have labored for Thee in
helpfulness to mankind, we give Thee grateful praise. In our
labors as we seek to serve Thee in building Thy holy city, give us
fidelity, courage, gentleness. Make us strong in Thy strength and
aglow with Thy Spirit, rejoicing in hope, patient in tribulation,
constant in prayer. So shall we render our best tribute to Thee
and to those who have blessed us with their building. Through
Jesus Christ our Lord. AMEN.

THE CRUSADER

Be steadfast, immovable, always abounding in the work of
the Lord, knowing that in the Lord your labor is not in vain.
—I Cor. 15:58 (R.S.V.)

Crusader for a happier, fairer world,
He speaks the truth with poignancy and power.
No carping word or slur can make him cower;
He bears no grudge when epithets are hurled.
For human good his ensign is unfurled.
He lives to make men love. When war clouds lower,
He points the way to harmony; when dour
Disaster stalks the earth, and men are whirled
Into a chaos of impending doom,
He speaks for change and will not acquiesce.
Defying prejudice and wonted wrong,
He helps to build tomorrow's world. No gloom
Disturbs his buoyancy, though burdens press.
He worships, toils, and waits—and he is strong.

We thank Thee, O God, for valiant souls of all the ages who, seeing a vision of Thy truth and holiness, have stood steadfast for Thee, and have proclaimed Thy righteous judgments against the evils of their time. Though smitten and outcast by men who preferred darkness to light and wonted ways to change, they have nevertheless wrought mightily for Thee. By their resolute effort has Thy kingdom been brought nearer. Into the heritage of their words and deeds we have come, and to them and to Thee we give grateful praise.

Give us in our time, O Lord, wisdom to discern what to do, courage to speak and to act, and grace from Thee to speak the truth in love. Accept our offering of ourselves for a better world in which men may deal more justly with one another, and in which oppression and strife may no longer curse the earth. Do with us as Thou wilt. Through Jesus Christ. AMEN.

TO A LITTLE BABY

[*Jesus*] *said to them, "Let the children come to me, do not hinder them; for to such belongs the kingdom of God." . . . And he took them in his arms and blessed them, laying his hands upon them.* —Mark 10:14, 16 (R.S.V.)

Sleep, little baby, sleep:
Your eyes are pools so deep
They hold God's mystery.
Now close them tight and see
What other realms there are
In dreams that grasp a star!
Sleep, little baby, sleep.

Sleep, little baby, sleep:
Let no dark shadow creep
Across your petaled face,
Alight with winsome grace.
Sleep well till morning's sun
Wakes you to merry fun!
Sleep, little baby, sleep.

We thank Thee, O God, for the sweet winsomeness of a baby's face, for its purity as it comes fresh from Thy hand, for the marvel and beauty of so great a gift from Thee.

Help us, O God, to love all children and to give them what they need to grow strong in body, mind, and soul. As Thy dear Son has hallowed all childhood with His blessing and favor, so may we see in every child, of whatever race or station, Thy divine image.

Thou hast taught us, "Blessed are the pure in heart, for they shall see God." Let the purity of a little child speak to us of that realm in which all is pure. Through our Christ who loved the children. AMEN.

VOICES OF GOD

And it shall come to pass afterward, that I will pour out
my spirit upon all flesh; and your sons and your daughters
shall prophesy, your old men shall dream dreams, your
young men shall see visions. —Joel 2:28

In speaking skies of silver, rose, and gold,
In circling rainbow hues, in grassy sward,
In stalwart mountain potencies, is told
    The glory of the Lord.

In joyous youth, alert, unstained, and free,
And faring forth to life's high heritage,
Is heard the song of those who, nerved by Thee,
    Set out on pilgrimage.

We praise and bless Thee, gracious Lord, for Thy radiant presence
in Thy world. Surpassing all the beauty of the earth is the beauty
of young lives. We rejoice that Thou hast placed it in the spirits of
youth to see visions of a new world, and to give themselves to
high adventure in the quest.

Take their buoyant energies, their eager aspiration, we pray,
and lead them in paths of Christian service in which their voices
shall be Thy voice. Show us how best we may encourage them
and guard us from putting impediments in their way. Give them
wisdom for the high responsibilities of the world they face, and
courage to go forward when there is much to confuse and daunt
them. Guide and sustain them, Lord, and direct us all as we seek
to help them. In the name of the young man Jesus we pray. AMEN.

TO A TEACHER

Receive my instruction, and not silver; and knowledge rather than choice gold. For wisdom is better than rubies; and all the things that may be desired are not to be compared to it. —Prov. 8:10-11

I thank our God for one who lived and taught
In wisdom's school, who ever walked with youth
And led the way in quest of timeless truth.
She scaled the rugged mountain heights of thought:
Keen was her mind—with gaze undimmed she sought
High verities, yet did not hold aloof
From simple folk or tasks. Her life was proof
Of her philosophy, in wholeness wrought.
She gave me words of counsel, was my friend;
I read her books, revered her from afar;
She helped me see life "steadily and whole."
She is not dead; such spirit cannot end.
She lives in me, and many. Naught can mar
The eternal radiance of a deathless soul.

We thank Thee, O Lord, for the great souls who have taught us in our growing years, and whose lives and minds have imparted gifts more precious than any earthly treasure. Help us in fidelity to Thee and in honor to them to seek to carry forward the heritage they gave us.

Direct and sustain all teachers, that by integrity of mind and heart they may show forth Thy truth. Help them to see their work as Thy calling. Open their eyes to the possibilities in those they teach, that they may bring forth the best in all young lives.

Send out, O Lord, Thy light and Thy truth; let them lead us. Instruct us in the spirit of wisdom and understanding, and endue us with that reverence for Thee which is the beginning of wisdom. Amen.

THEY ALSO SERVE

Having eyes do you not see, and having ears do you not hear? —Mark 8:18 (R.S.V.)

> To dwell in darkness all the years—
>   And yet see light,
> To look not on another's face—
>   And yet have sight,
> To see by love the hidden things
>   I do not see,
> Such seeing of the inner eye
>   Shows Christ to me.
>
> To look serenely on the world
>   Nor rail at fate,
> To live believing that they serve
>   Who stand and wait,
> To labor, walking in the way
>   The saints have trod,
> Such courage lights the way for me
>   And shows me God.

We thank Thee, Lord, for eyes to see a world Thou hast made so beautiful. Even more we thank Thee for what a soul attuned to Thy Spirit can behold.

That men though blind or maimed in body can yet live nobly is Thy good gift. Beholding this victory, we who have suffered no such loss are challenged to deeper feeling and purer living. Help us, Lord, to use to Thy glory the sound bodies that too often ungratefully we have accepted from Thee as our due, and when they are impaired let us still praise Thee for Thy good gifts.

Above all, O Lord, with the inner eye let us see Thee as Thou art, that we may serve Thee with fullness of joy. AMEN.

EVENSONG

At evening time there shall be light. —Zech. 14:7 (R.S.V.)

When Time's unstaying hour hand makes its way
Toward twelve, and when the clear red buoyancy
That youth bequeathed to middle life turns gray,
When firm step halts and eye does not quite see,
Then may I walk with steadfast step and sure,
Upborne by inner strength that cannot fail;
Then may I face with flame within still pure
The years, or timelessness, beyond the veil.

So would I live, and there are those I know
Who mark the way. Their threescore years and ten
Are like an altar lit with mellow glow,
The life a prayer, and now the rich Amen.
Within such hallowed presence I can feel
The touch of Him who died on Calvary.
His radiant, deathless youth He gave to heal
The wounds of age and set such spirits free.

Almighty God, before whom the generations rise and pass away, we thank Thee for all the gifts of Thy wise providence. For the strength of youth and the high opportunities of the middle years we thank Thee, but beyond these for the mellowed wisdom and ripe fruitage of old age.

We rejoice, O God, that our lives have been blessed and our souls warmed by those rich in years in whom Thy image shines undimmed. As they have loved and labored for others in kindliness and cheer, so would we live. As they have been faithful to Thee, so would we be steadfast. Go with them, Lord, through the days of failing strength and the shadows of the parting into the glory and joy of Thine eternal kingdom. Then when our years come to grow old and in Thy good time to pass beyond the veil, wilt Thou sustain us to the end and take us to dwell in Thy nearer presence. Through Christ our great Companion. AMEN.

THE QUEST

Blessed is the man whose strength is in thee;
In whose heart are the highways to Zion.
Passing through the valley of Weeping they make it a place
of springs;
Yea, the early rain covereth it with blessings.

—Ps. 84:5-6 (A.S.V.)

If in the press of every day
The holy chalice slips away;
If in the treadmill of my toil
My lamps are dry of festal oil;
If in the desert waste of things
I find no wells, no limpid springs:
    Lord, touch with dew my parching heart,
    Anoint it ere it crack apart.

If in my own felicity
I walk as one who does not see;
If in a tangled underbrush
I move, and know not what I crush;
If in an avalanche of care
I use not mountain-moving prayer;
    Grant me no highway to the Grail—
    But light me, Lord, to find a trail.

Almighty God our Father, Companion of the daily road, we humbly confess before Thee that we do not always sense Thy nearness. Pressed upon by duties and demands, tired in body and dull in soul, we let the awareness of Thy presence slip away. Then as we try to walk alone, we stumble and fall.

Lift us up, O God, and set us again on the road with our hands in Thine. Give us zest for living and zeal for serving, and make us strong in the assurance that we are not called to strive by might or by power, but by Thy Spirit. Then as we pass through our valleys of weeping, help us by Thy strength to transform them into springs whence living waters flow. Through Christ our Lord. AMEN.

A PRAYER FOR WISDOM

Happy is the man that findeth wisdom,
And the man that getteth understanding.
For the gaining of it is better than the gaining of silver,
And the profit thereof than fine gold.

—Prov. 3:13-14 (A.S.V.)

Grant me today this prayer:
I would have beauty, Lord,
Not beauty of the outward form,
Not fine array to deck my flesh,
But beauty absolute,
God's comeliness within—
That beauty of the inward soul
For which the wise man prayed to Pan.

Like Socrates, I too
Would have the life within
At one with that I show to men—
My treasure wisdom, and my gold
No more than may the wise
In health of soul possess.
Is there aught else, O Lord, to ask?
This is my prayer. It is enough.

Eternal and all-wise God, who hast revealed Thyself to the seers of all the ages, grant us true wisdom in our time. We bless Thee for the heritage of learning that has been placed in our hands through the earnest seeking of men of many generations. Let us be worthy of this gift.

We pray Thee, O God, for inward purity. Let Thy Spirit cleanse our hearts and quicken our sight to behold and follow what is good and true and beautiful.

We pray Thee, Lord, for open minds. Help us without reluctance or fear to apprehend new truth and to guard unspoiled the treasure committed to us. In gratitude to Thee and to those who have gone before, help us to carry forward the lamps they lighted and use them to Thy glory. AMEN.

ABIDE IN ME

If you abide in me, and my words abide in you, ask whatever you will, and it shall be done for you.

—John 15:7 (R.S.V.)

Lord Christ, who came from God to make men free,
Come Thou into my heart, lift even me.

Lord Christ, our Saviour in this world of strife,
Help me to do Thy will: purge Thou my life.

Lord Christ, our Beacon in the darkest night,
Guide Thou my steps, my Leader and my Light.

Lord Christ, our Comrade of the daily task,
Walk with me in the way: no more I ask.

Our Lord Christ, we would abide in Thee, and seek to let Thy words abide in us, as each new morning comes with its storehouse of joys and responsibilities. We would abide in Thee amid the pressures and strains of our daily tasks. We would abide in Thee as the shadows fall, and the evening comes, and we go to our rest. In Thee we would lie down in peace of soul, and be made strong for the new day.

As we enter that longer night which leads to day in Thine eternal kingdom, still we would abide in Thee and trust Thy loving hand. And in all we ask, O Christ, let Thy words abide in us. AMEN.

O GOD MOST HOLY

*And suddenly there was with the angel a multitude of
the heavenly host praising God and saying,
"Glory to God in the highest,
and on earth peace among men with whom he is pleased!"*
—Luke 2:13-14 (R.S.V.)

O God most holy, God most high,
Who came to earth in a baby's cry,
Though hearts be troubled, dark with fear,
Where Thou dost reign there reigneth cheer.
Come Thou to us; be Thou our King;
Come now and let rejoicing ring.

O Jesus Lord of heaven and earth,
Sweet Mary's child of a lowly birth,
Thy glory gleams above men's might;
Where Thou dost come there cometh light.
Dwell Thou today within my heart;
Come Thou and nevermore depart.

Almighty and eternal God, who hast come to live among men in
the child of Bethlehem and the man of Galilee, come Thou near
and dwell among us.

Preserve us, O God, in our bodies and in our souls, that we may
be fit dwelling places of Thy Spirit. Let our hearts be clear of
offense, our acts without stain. So may our lives praise Thee.

We would worship Thee, O Lord, in spirit and in truth, by our
words and by our deeds. Again let the heavens resound and the
earth be glad in praises to Thy glory. Anew amid our strife-torn
world, let peace be born among men whose deeds are pleasing unto
Thee.

For Thy best gift to earth we have no return to offer, save to
give Thee ourselves. Use us as Thou wilt, and grant us Thy peace.
AMEN.

SHED THOU, O LORD, THY LIGHT

Blessed is the nation whose God is the Lord.
$\qquad$ —Ps. 33:12 (R.S.V.)

Tune: *Bread of Life*

Shed Thou, O Lord, Thy light
On this strong land.
Firm in the ways of right,
Strong may she stand.
Make her to all earth kin,
Teach her to share;
Cleanse her of inward sin;
Lord, hear our prayer.

Purge Thou from pride her life;
Stay lust for gain;
Save from unholy strife;
Let justice reign.
Make her Thine instrument
To bring earth peace,
Good will her armament
Till wars shall cease.

Here let all men be free
Under Thy sun,
Bound in fraternity,
All peoples one.
Here let Thy truth be power,
All deeds be just.
Save, Lord, in this grave hour;
In Thee we trust.[1]

We thank Thee, O God, for the great heritage of a free land dedicated to ideals of liberty and justice for all. Help us more faithfully to serve Thee through serving it. Under Thy righteous leading, may it lead the way for all nations to security, justice, and peace. AMEN.

[1] Copyright 1945 by the Hymn Society of America for inclusion in *Hymns of Christian Patriotism*. Used by permission.

93

WORD OF LIFE

Thy word is a lamp to my feet
and a light to my path.
>   —Ps. 119:105 (R.S.V.)

Tune: *Materna*

Thy Word, O God, the Book of Life,
   That tells Thy will and way,
Let this be now a beacon light
   Upon our stricken day.
When nations quake and systems shake,
   Here find our souls release;
Within this Book the longer look
   Brings vistas of Thy peace.

For here is told the best we know
   Of wisdom, faith and good;
The story of Thy Father-love
   Is seed of brotherhood.
In Thy command our duty lies,
   In Christ our goal we see;
Our freedom and our strength are won
   Through Him who makes us free.

Be Thou, O Lord, from sacred page
   A lamp unto our feet.
As Thou hast led our fathers forth,
   So may we scorn retreat.
To Thee, O God, we pledge our all,
   Heart, soul, and strength and mind;
In Christ our Lord known through Thy Word
   Thy saving health to find.

We rejoice, O God, that in Thy holy Word Thou dost tell us all
we need to know of Thee. By it Thou dost call us to repent of
our sin; Thou dost promise forgiveness; Thou dost set before us
the way of life. Thou hast shown us the way; give us grace to
walk in it. In Christ's name. AMEN.

STRONG DEFENSE

He only is my rock and my salvation.—Ps. 62:2 (R.S.V.)

King of glory, Lord, we hail Thee,
Thou art our eternal Friend;
Men may flout Thy ways, assail Thee,
Thou art faithful to the end.
Forward Thou hast led the ages
Over many a cragged way;
Strong defense through fateful stages,
Wilt Thou fail us in our day?

Dark the hour and cleft the nations,
Grim the swirling tides of fear;
High above earth's habitations
Is Thy realm, and Thou art near—
Nearer than our faintest murmur,
Closer than our darkest mood;
Rifts are deep, Thy bands are firmer,
Drawing men to men for good.

Light shone forth in benediction
From Thy Son our Lord Christ's face,
Shrinking not from crucifixion,
Risen still He shows Thy grace.
Works of men grow stale and crumble,
Fruitless are the ways of strife;
Trusting Him we shall not stumble,
Christ the Way, the Truth, the Life.

Out of the depths, O Lord, we cry unto Thee. Save us lest we perish in our own indifference and despair. Forgive our iniquities; strengthen us for our labors; confirm us in a faith that cannot be shaken. Through Jesus Christ our Lord. AMEN.

MY HANDIWORK

And let the beauty of the Lord our God be upon us: and establish thou the work of our hands upon us; yea, the work of our hands establish thou it. —Ps. 90:17

My handiwork, O Lord, establish Thou.
I would not toil and strive just for the now.
Within my heart is set eternity.
I would fulfill the quest that is of Thee.

The daily round of things shuts out the light.
How fleeting seems the gain! How soon comes night!
I long to do great works: I beat the air.
My soul is buffeted with each day's care.

And yet—my daily task is Thy behest!
I will not let its bonds hold back my quest;
Its ties shall bind me fast and set me free.
With vision of Thy goals then I shall see.

If what I do today be wrought in prayer,
The fruit is in Thy hands, for Thou art there
Beside my path. Our Father, lead me now;
My handiwork, O Lord, establish thou.

God of the daily task, who didst send Thy blessed Son to live among men as a working man, help us to be faithful in the labors Thou hast entrusted to our hands. Help us to find Thy will and Thy work in the humblest task as in the greatest, and make us quick to answer when Thou callest.

Make us alert to find Thee ever near. Speak through the confusion of our too hurried and anxious lives, made fretful by petty annoyances and the monotonous routine of things that must be done, and help us to be still enough to hear Thy voice. Give us wisdom and strength for the day's work and help us to see all our labor as a service done to Thee. Then when our work on earth is done, gather us to Thine eternal kingdom to serve Thee there as Thou desirest. Through Christ our Lord. AMEN.